EXACTING CLAM No. 18 — AUTUMN 2025

CONTENTS

Front cover: "Thinking of Max" by Mike Silverton
© 2025 Sagging Meniscus Press
All Rights Reserved
ISBN: 978-1-963846-57-7 (paperback)
 978-1-963846-58-4 (ebook)
exactingclam.com
Exacting Clam is a quarterly publication from Sagging Meniscus.
Contributing Editors: Jake Goldsmith, Tomoé Hill, Kurt Luchs,
 Melissa McCarthy, M.J. Nicholls, Mike Silverton, Thomas Walton

Contributing Metaclamician: Christopher Boucher
Senior Editors: Jeff Chon, Elizabeth Cooperman, Tyler C. Gore,
 Doug Nufer
Fiction Editor: Charles Holdefer
Poetry Editor: Aaron Anstett
Reviews Editor: Jesi Bender
Assistant Editor: Gina DeMartino
Executive Editor: Guillermo Stitch
Publisher: Jacob Smullyan

Jake Goldsmith

On Annoyance

Annoyance is a milder emotion than big-otry, and we are often terribly annoyed by the manner and attitudes of friends and people we agree with. Annoyance often derives from a discomfort between an undesired voice, a presence or action, and an agreeable or desired environment—or perhaps better said: it is an unwanted distraction from conscious thought or a preferred atmosphere. I am most annoyed by my friends and family, not my enemies. I want to explore the manner in which I too am annoying, and why I, personally, am annoyed at so many things all the time. I will keep this grumpiness brief and not write anything substantial . . . to avoid annoyance.

Perhaps my curtness will be found annoying.

How I have written this article may be a source of annoyance to those who prefer certain styles, but let's put that aside for now. No matter what literary, journalistic, formal or informal style this is written in, it is bound to annoy *someone*.

I was vaguely annoyed when I learnt about the existence of formal, academic 'Annoyance' and 'Boredom' studies, declared professional disciplines. Given no prior knowledge, I thought immediately, with a knee-jerk prejudice, that this was some sort of over-scrupulous, positivist, scientistic systematising of a concept that is too diffuse and obscure to be confidently ordered; just as I might view psychology or economics. I was annoyed at the new knowledge, and then annoyed at myself for my dismissiveness.

What's particular, or peculiar, about my sense of annoyance is how curmudgeonly wide-ranging it is. It is not that I cultivate any particular hatred for most of what enters my realm to piss me off, as hatred would require more energy and might be construed as a compliment in reverse, but my austere disrespect for all ages and classes and faces can still be acute in each instance; where a lofty distaste for anti-intellectual delinquents rests in bed, in some freakish versatile coitus, with disdain for snobbish intellectuals.

Particular eccentricities are tedious. Eccentricities that appear as an organic part of one's person are tolerated, but these are hard to come by, like striving for authenticity if one is trying too hard. Odd things can be delightful, but many won't find them so. Oddities in fashion or manner are tolerable if one isn't trying; like *Sprezzatura*, the Italian art of effortless grace, which is to say, making the difficult easy. Otherwise, eccentricities in behaviour or presentation appear *affected*. Affectations are fine in jest but not as part of everyday character. Many possess affected manners, through insecurity, wanting to stand out or stand in, or to distinguish themselves in some way, though most such signs cause judgement or contempt. It is hard to suggest how to avoid this. Someone somewhere will always find any particular thought or action personally offensive due to their own idiosyncrasies, even if what they object to is good, but we can mostly forget people like that. The mild suggestion might be to try to be more comfortable in one's own skin, and as such find less reason to affect our style and conduct, though that is a lot to ask.

Depending on your mood, all of the above may be found annoying (as if I am anyone to suggest anything), and can be dismissed. Or aesthetics alone may be reason enough: as maybe my writing is *affected*, even if I'm mostly a sort of chameleon naturally adopting elements from what I've read. Regardless, that too can be uncomfortable. It still might seem like an imposition. Or I might easily be a bore. Too often I find the over-committed, the overcertain, those too full of passionate intensity, to be the most annoying. They are particularly overzealous in their certainty despite the sparseness of their reading, or the surplus of time they have spent skulking around social media. Yet—with a rejoinder anyone observant enough might predict—those who seem the opposite of the former, which is to say, more aloof, too ambivalent, apathetic and careless, are similarly irritating. It is a commitment to superfluous intransigence, the hateful, closed and locked-down kind, that damages most. To be committed but open, with few truly settled convictions (especially in firmly academic philosophy), yet still having strong views . . . is not a contradiction. It is too easy to be committed but closed. Few approach this kind of moderation, I can hardly be said to do so, and it is annoying that we are so inept. A lesson I should probably learn is to accept, in some part, while remaining posed against our inherent human unreasonableness. This is far easier to accept as an abstract intellectual position than as an immediate feeling. There is a real danger in being too cautious, but I usually prefer it to being too bold—or arrogant . . . and therefore annoying.

The smartest or most accomplished can be terrible people, or at least too smug and overbearing, hence annoying. Lesser people, not as morally sound or brilliant, can make better friends and prove more reliable in both everyday or desperate situations. Some of the greatest minds in history have been annoying personalities. The polymath Gottfried Wilhelm Leibniz, for all his many accomplishments and creative excellence, was known to be confident to the point of great immodesty, socially awkward, boastful and exaggerative. Being skillful and technically gifted mean less to many if one is clumsy and patronising. The arrogant may protest, thinking the substance of their work is enough, yet neglecting tact, good taste and good form makes life difficult. Their superiority is detested even more so for being vulgar, and success would be more forthcoming if great yet vain and egotistical people were more discerning and socially aware—hence less annoying.

What I find most annoying about myself is my impulsiveness. I can rarely defer any need for quick satisfaction or comfort, though thankfully only with respect to minor vices. The major ones are too physically tiresome or distant; too annoying to even begin. I am sensitive to change and to sincerely rude behaviour, and I am emotionally fragile as well as physically frail. People comment on an apparent stoicism I display in the light of morbid subjects, but this front soon fails. I am quick to lose my cool and become temperamental, and I overshare. This is my natural disposition, and it is frustrating. Becoming a more prudent person able to better cope with the world's vices *and* my own is onerous.

Ideally, I should aim to find myself less annoying, if only for the sake of my own health, while annoyance at the outside world is not always so bad. It may be unhealthy, or hurtful, but a banal and obvious truth worth stating is that exasperation is a sure indication that something is wrong. It is hard to begrudge ourselves when we instinctually become animated and rude, even in an annoying way, or in an ineffective way, as the world, society, our institutions, give us sufficient cause to be distrustful or upset. The fact that the world is currently becoming less just, more unsafe, less trusting or trustworthy, is more than a source of annoyance. It is a reason for deep concern. Annoyance is doubled when we react incapably. Unfortunately the world and its denizens will only become more annoying in time, though this may give others an opportunity to be less annoying. Observe the most risible features of your country, class, age, nationality, etc, and work to avoid them. Their absence will merit you a hearty congratulation. Yet if too much effort is put into avoiding annoyances, the inevitable irony rises again.

Annoyance is inescapable. I used the words *annoying, annoyance,* or *annoy* at least 39 times in this essay. I fear repetition without good context is a common annoyance. And now, I find myself unable to end these thoughts in a nonannoying way.

Kurt Luchs

Hunting Everything But Pheasants With Robert Bly

In some ways, the place of Robert Bly in our literature during his heyday can be compared to that of Ezra Pound during his. Pound was the leader and the center of the revolution in American and English poetry that took place in the early decades of the last century. The circumstances were unique and unlikely to ever be repeated. In any case, they haven't been. The number of poets and literary journals that mattered was small, and he knew them all. Even the ones who despised him—and there were more than a few, as noted by Robert Frost, who referred to Pound's "gentle art of making enemies"—were influenced by him, almost against their will, such was the power of his personality and his passion for poetry. Though Yeats was twenty years his senior, Pound paradoxically mentored him into the new age and was certainly a key influence on his later and best work. Pound could befriend both T.S. Eliot and William Carlos Williams, living symbols of the clash between formalism and free verse who didn't like or understand each other (the best book about that is *Three on the Tower* by Louis Simpson). As the facsimile edition of "The Waste Land" made plain, it was Pound who gave that famous poem its final form.

Robert Bly also led a revolution in our poetry several generations later, though by then the world of poetry was so fragmented that no one figure, not even Bly, could command the influence once wielded by Pound. By the time Bly came on the scene in the 1950s, the poetry revolution of the early twentieth century had become the establishment. Large swathes of the literary scene consisted of poets trying to out-Eliot Eliot, such as Robert Lowell, or to out-Auden Auden, such as Howard Nemerov. The leading magazines had become dull and predictable, not unlike today. Clearly, another revolution was needed.

Several were already in motion, in fact. While the permanent worth of some of the Beatniks' work will continue to be debated (and I'm a bit of a doubter myself, as I doubt almost everything), there's no denying they brought poetry back into popular culture and public consciousness. They made live poetry readings a vogue again. They affiliated themselves with the most intelligent popular music of the time, jazz. And finally, they made it acceptable to write political poems again, as it had not been since the 1930s. That's all in their favor.

At the same time, a very different revolution was being led by the New York school of poets, with John Ashbery, Kenneth Koch, Frank O'Hara and James Schuyler at the fore. They had in common with the Beats a sense of humor. Where the Beats tended to act the clown in public, or perhaps more fairly to be seen as jesters, the New York poets were wits and proudly sophisticated and international in their tastes. Both groups were inveterate pranksters. Even James Dickey, who never liked any Beat poet ever, enjoyed the sharp yet humane humor of Ginsberg.

The thing is, these divisions were almost total on the literary as well as the personal level. These groups did not mix much. They tended to share a mutual contempt for each other and the establishment. Each had their own magazines and anthologies, and when they deigned to review the work outside their own cliques they would spit venom like cobras. How funny it all seems now. And how different from today, when there are no schools of poetry worthy of the name, not even to ridicule, and practically nobody dares give a book a bad review. Poetry may still be half-alive (again, I am dubious), but criticism is deader than the Lindbergh baby.

But to return to Mr. Bly. The third poetic revolution, the one he led, was a rebellion against the stuffy, academic, denatured verse that dominated the establishment poets of the fifties. Against all odds, some of these poets still managed to write good poems. Lowell may be a waste of space, for example, but Nemerov is actually well worth reading. Overall, however, the Beats, the New York poets and the less definable school led by Bly had a point. Poetry had in some essential way gone off the rails. Or maybe the problem was the opposite: poetry had become too tame and timidly stayed in its own little lane, not greatly affected by or affecting anything else.

This too sounds very similar to our current situation.

Bly recognized the problem and sought to correct it in several ways. He understood that formalism had been exhausted and ruined as a technique, at least for the moment, for most poets, so he pushed for a free verse revolution. The Beats were in complete agreement of course, the New York poets not so much. Especially Koch, who showed that a dead formalism can be revived at any time by infusing it with life, love and laughter.

Secondly, Bly grasped that American poets needed to look for inspiration and models outside of their immediate past and their country's borders. For him and many others in his circle, this mostly meant digging into the work of the great Hispanic poets such as Lorca, Neruda, Machado, Jimenez, Borges, Hernandez, Vallejo, Mistral, etc. Meanwhile the New York poets looked mainly to the French, and the Beats, apart from understandably idolizing Whitman, looked outside of literature altogether.

Finally, Bly and his fellow travelers wanted to focus less on verbal pyrotechnics and more on what he called the "subjective image" (others called it the "deep image"), the mysterious, dreamlike, nonreducible heart of the poem. Some of his leading fellow travelers, not necessarily always in agreement with his program or his poetics, included James Wright, W. S. Merwin, Louis Simpson and John Logan, among others. Notice that it was a boy's club. Many things were back then. One of the positive changes about the current poetry scene is that for the first time ever, most of the best poets are women, of which Ada Limon is an excellent exemplar.

Both Bly and Logan edited magazines, two of the most significant and useful of their time. Bly started the *Fifties*, which became the *Sixties* and then the *Seventies*. It never got to the *Eighties*, but by then his work of reconstruction was done. Logan helmed *Choice*, which, among other things, published Bly's groundbreaking and controversial essay, "A Wrong Turning in American Poetry." We are badly in need of a sequel to that. I could write it myself, but I won't, because what happened to Bly after he wrote his manifesto—a successful revolution—is not what would happen to me. Nothing would change except that I would be canceled and doxed and never heard from again, my career in literature (or at least in poetry) over forever. The sad truth is that I kind of want to get somewhere in this business before they send me to the (hopefully metaphorical) guillotine. Yes, I am a moral and intellectual coward. I'm not proud of it, but there it is.

Well, that's enough of a preamble for any poetic career and any poem! The Bly poem under discussion today is "Hunting Pheasants in a Cornfield," from his first full-length collection *Silence in the Snowy Fields* (Wesleyan 1962), issued when he was thirty-six. He had waited a while to publish. In that sense most of his contemporaries were way ahead of him, especially Merwin, a year younger than him, who already had four books under his belt and the fifth, his own groundbreaker *The Moving Target*, coming in 1963. Bly's delay was intentional, however. He felt that a poet shouldn't put out a book until he was at least thirty and knew who he (or she) was. He didn't wait quite as long as one of his heroes, Wallace Stevens, whose first volume *Harmonium* came in 1923 when he was forty-four. Just for comparison, ponder the fact that by the time Keats was forty-four he had been dead for eighteen years.

For Bly, the wait was worth it. This is a man who knows what he knows. *Silence in the Snowy Fields* feels confident and assured without being arrogant, fresh without straining for novelty. The poems are all short, none of them more than a page. Half a dozen of them are only five lines or less. At seventeen lines, "Hunting Pheasants in a Cornfield" is one of the longer poems here. It is divided into four numbered stanzas, the first three consisting of four lines each and the last one containing five.

The first thing to notice about it is that the pheasants appear only in the title, and by implication in the last line. In other words, the title tells us what brought him to the cornfield. The poem tells us what he found there, starting in stanza one:

> What is so strange about a tree alone in an open field?
> It is a willow tree. I walk around and around it.
> The body is strangely torn, and cannot leave it.
> At last I sit down beneath it.

He thought he was hunting pheasants, yet it's almost as if the tree was hunting him. He has been completely captured by it. As John Lennon says in the song "Beautiful Boy," "Life is what happens when we're busy making other plans." At this point the poet is not even fully conscious of what is happening. It's his body that is "strangely torn," not his mind. Although he doesn't mention what he's wearing or carrying, the season and the activity mean he must have on an overcoat and be holding a shotgun. One of the subtlest effects of the poem is how the tree disarms him without it ever being openly acknowledged that he is armed (a man sitting like Buddha beneath a willow tree is not thinking about his shotgun). And isn't this what all great art does? It takes us by surprise, peels back our protections and takes us out of ourselves and whatever we thought we were doing.

Stanza two pays more attention to specifics about the tree, showing that the poet's mind has become engaged with the mysterious attraction. He notes that the willow is totally isolated in "acres of dry corn." The second line plays a key role, as it will have a sequel in the final stanza: "Its leaves are scattered around its trunk, and around me." Bly has become one with the tree, if only in his imagination, in order to find out what's going on. Ever the carefully observant naturalist, he sees that the tree's fallen brown leaves are "speckled with delicate black." Little dots of death, perhaps? When he says in the last line of the stanza, "Only the cornstalks now can make a noise", he tells us that the wind blows through the remains of the corn and reminds us that the tree is not only alone but silent. Just as he is.

Suddenly in stanza three he makes one of those characteristic Robert Bly leaps (recall that he edited an anthology called *Leaping Poetry*), speaking of the cold winter sun "burning through the frosty distances of space." I believe this is his way of tying the tree's aloneness and his own to the loneliness of planet Earth. The word "death," which has been hovering at the fringes of the poem, gets said out loud for the first and only time when he mentions the dead frozen weeds in line two of this stanza. The conclusion of stanza three puts these things together to give a particular spin to his fascination with the tree: "Why then do I love to watch / The sun moving on the chill skin of the branches?" Why indeed? The sun cannot warm during this frozen hunting season. But it can still illuminate, like the awakened mind. And now we are ready for stanza four:

The mind has shed leaves alone for years.
It stands apart with small creatures near its roots.
I am happy in this ancient place,
A spot easily caught sight of above the corn,
If I were a young animal ready to turn home at dusk.

With the first line of this stanza the implicit identification of the poet with the tree has finally been made explicit. The mind "stands apart," as all minds must, though ironically it can only think by means of likenesses; for instance, how it is like a tree, or the sun. It is meaningful that this poem falls in the first section of the book, which is called "Eleven Poems of Solitude" (fyi, the other two sections are called "Awakening" and "Silence on the Roads"). Why is it worth mentioning that the tree in the cornfield is an "ancient place"? And why should it make him happy? Not everything in a poem needs a reason to exist other than beauty and the joy it gives. But I think this is partly his indirect way of letting us know this is a massive willow, a very old tree that spreads both up and out. It's a landmark in the physical world as is his encounter with it in his mind and memory.

The last line of the stanza, and the poem, seems to bring us back to the pheasants that Bly thought he was hunting at the beginning, calling the place of the tree "A spot easily caught sight of above the corn, / If I were a young animal ready to turn home at dusk." Now, nobody goes pheasant hunting at dusk, not if they want to avoid an awkward Dick Cheney moment with the shotgun. In his quiet, oblique way, Bly is giving us an idea of how long he's been sitting under that tree like a Zen apprentice. He would've gone hunting no later than the afternoon, which means it's been hours at least. I find it interesting that he no longer mentions the pheasants by name, as if they aren't on his hit list anymore. And they aren't, because he now identifies with them too. He refers instead to a generic "young animal." In a way, this underscores the feeling the poem leaves us with, of the oneness of all life.

Parting note to young poets, or any poets young at heart: they tell you there are rules for writing, like "avoid the passive voice" and "always be specific." But in truth there are no rules except the tacit rules of intelligence and taste and instinct for what is right in the moment and right for the poem, which often demand that we break the so-called rules. If Bly had listened to the self-appointed rule-makers instead of his own inner spirit, he never could have created this marvelous poem. He never would have set out to hunt pheasants and ended up hunting enlightenment under a bare willow.

KURT LUCHS

THE BOULDER

The boulder was not magnetic and yet
it drew us to the creek bed
where it sat beside the dark waters
while we sat on it and looked and listened

I say the waters were dark but really
they were clear the darkness
was in the moss rippling beneath them
as if to the tinkling gurgling music rushing past

The granite stone was more than a stool
for beings who did not exist when it was born
it was a gallery with a single exhibit
revealing just how much beauty could be wrought

by pure randomness with no visible artist
the quartz and feldspar flecked with mica
shining even in the shade of the giant cottonwood
inviting eyes and fingers to explore

or simply to rest silently soaking it in
This was the place we came to when our father
tired of hitting us and we slunk away
to be alone or alone together

and to be soothed by the sound of the waters
and the sure presence of the boulder
something older and stronger than us
with no desire to harm us

Occasionally the glint of the mica
would be answered by the flashing scales
of a bluegill swimming furiously against the current
so much energy spent to remain in one place

yes what I'm saying is he was one of us
perhaps also drawn by the boulder's mysterious power
it never would have occurred to us
to try to capture or kill him

There were other places to pause
fallen branches and the chain-sawed stump
of another cottonwood but still the glittering
boulder was always the only choice

and how strange that I should be there right now
though it no longer exists except far down inside me
which may be how what disappears
lives on and the dark waters keep flowing flowing

Melissa McCarthy

Category Errors

Creature : garment

The orcas wear a salmon hat, is the summer 2025 dispatch on shenanigans in the ocean world. They—the grampi, *Orciduses*, bad mammals—apparently clown around by finding a salmon, balancing it on their sinister, flat-topped heads, and cavorting. We're not sure if it's a fashion trend, or a decoy to attract more poor fish into the gloating jaws, or just for the ghoulish pleasure. Uncertain, too, if the salmon is definitely dead, or if it's terrified or coerced into silence and immobility, before the besporting starts. It's hard to fathom the motivation.

Human : animal

Let's loop back a little to the Circe episode in Homer's *Odyssey*, book 10 (the one before the Book of the Dead) as recounted by the eponymous hero. He and his men have left Aeolia and got back to within sight of Ithaca, only to mess up with the bag of winds, and suffer at the hands of the man-eating Laestrygonians. Just one shipfull of men, weary and tearful, is left. They pitch up in an island and see red smoke coming from a fine, polished palace in the middle. Half the crew make an exploring party, knock on the door, and are welcomed in by the goddess Circe. She gives them fine food, but, as the 1946 Rieu translation says, "she introduced a noxious drug, to make them lose all memory of their native land. [. . .] Now they had pigs' heads and bristles, and they grunted like pigs; but their minds were as human as they had been before. So, weeping, they were penned in their sties."

Eating : carrying

Odysseus feels obliged to set out for the palace on a rescue mission, rejecting his crew-mate's exhortation to just flee, with the decisive statement, "I shall go. I have absolutely no choice." On his way, he encounters Hermes, who presents him with a pre-antidote to Circe's poison; it will make him immune to Circe's drug, and Odysseus must then extract promises of good behaviour from Circe before sleeping with her. That's the helpful advice from the messenger god. It's interesting that though many other moments of action from this chapter are told or even repeated in detail, the exact mechanism and process of this counteracting plant are a little vague. Hermes explains, "here is a drug of real virtue that you must take with you into Circe's palace," and Odysseus says that Hermes "handed me a herb he had plucked from the ground, and showed me what it was like. It had a black root and a milk-white flower. The gods call it moly, and it is a dangerous plant for mortal men to dig up. But the gods, after all, can do anything." That's it; there's no close-up of him ingesting the plant. It looks as though he just has to carry it with him, this black-and-white preventative, prophylactic plant.

Hermes' plan goes as stated. Odysseus shows admirable prioritisation by obeying Circe's instruction to "come with me to my bed, so that in making love we may learn to trust one another," but on the other hand he's too upset to eat, until she agrees to reinstate the men. She smears them with "some new ointment. Then the bristles which her first deadly potion had caused to sprout dropped off their limbs, and they became men again and looked younger and much more handsome and taller than before."

Everyone is pleased; the Ithacans stay there for a whole year, feasting and resting. Then all the crew want to get home; Odysseus agrees, and Circe concurs, saying only that they must first go down to Hades to confirm directions. This whole Circe adventure is not the worst, for the Greeks. Odysseus enjoys it. Only one sailor, Elpenor, falls off a roof and dies. The others have a pig adventure, but recover.

Bad days : good days

As well as classical literature (my regular readers might have divined by now), I'm interested in translation, and in proverbs and turns of phrase, from various languages. A recent Spanish one that pleased me was, *a cada cerdo llega su San*

Martín—to each pig arrives his or her own Saint Martin. Saint Martin's day, 11th November, was widely celebrated around Europe as a festival day marking the end of harvest and the onset of winter. There would be celebrations, bonfires, wine-cracking, and, to help with the feasting, the slaughtering of a *cerdo*, or pig.

At first glance I assumed that the phrase was similar to the English one, "every dog has his day," with its positive overtones of, we will all be celebrated at some point, get our hour in the sun. Or, if you were feeling foolishly optimistic, you could read the proverb in a cheerful way, that even a pig gets to join in the party. But really, it means that the day of your own personal come-uppance will come, you'll get what's coming to you, one day. You have fucked around, and you will find out. A no-nonsense consequence.

Pig : sailor

Luckily, things don't go as badly as this, not just now, for Odysseus' men. They are reconstituted, recovered, healed, by Circe's second ointment. We don't know what this is: is it the same as the moly that Hermes presents? Surely of the same pharmaceutical group, able to repel and/or revoke the effect of the piggification poison. I'm interested that they return to their human form younger, more handsome and taller than before—the experience has perhaps frightened them but has improved them (from a conventional dating perspective). Also we don't really know what moly is—a magic herb with a black root and white flower. Sort of orca-coloured.

Spanish : isiZulu

There's another language that for residential purposes I've dabbled in, which is isiZulu, one of South Africa's national languages. What's the word for "shark," I of course wanted to learn. One is *imfingo*, a "species of dark-colored shark" (says *English-Zulu Zulu-English Dictionary*, Wits UP, 1990). *Imfingo* also means, a "medicine used for counteracting a harmful charm." This is cool. (*Isifingo*, "deep darkness preceding the dawn," likewise.) So this is what Hermes presents to Odysseus to keep about his person (it seems), to stop Circe being able to translate him into a pig: the monochrome moly, which is imfingo. Looking further, the noun comes from the verb *finga*, meaning, "to render harmless, destroy the virtue of a harmful charm", and, as a second definition, "to cause to forget, dull the memory." There's a lot of excellent concepts swimming about in the same etymological pool, here.

Remembering : forgetting

I like this from the isiZulu, the fact that the same word applies for making harmless, stopping it hurting, and, making someone forget. Imfingo, the thing that heals, by this linguistic chain of associations, is, forgetting. Letting it go, moving on in your voyage. If something hurts, the way to heal it is by forgetting. Or, there's another common recommendation: time, as the healer. But who wants to wait. Odysseus' men, fed up with the lap of luxury, prompt him to get going, not to dally longer. "It's time you thought of Ithaca." (I'd prefer it if they had said, how can you forget your homeland like this, but I have to admit, they don't.)

But there's one snag about the sailors and their memories. Odysseus says that Circe first drugged them "to make them lose all memory of their native land." That's fine, but we're also told that "their minds were as human as they had been before." So which is it: that they carry on, essentially the same as before but just trapped in pig bodies; or, that they turn outwardly porcine and they have no memory of before, of home. In that sense, then, though, in what way are they still human? It's so much of who we are. The past, the memories. Even the painful ones.

And, they don't permanently forget, as we can tell by the fact that when they're back as humans they want to leave, home for Ithaca. I don't think Homer has it quite right: with Circe's first ointment (yes ok oinkment) the sailors don't actually forget, they've just changed a bit. They are trapped in these bodies but internally the same, and the forgetting phrase is not factually about amnesia but is a turn of phrase or a metaphor meaning, I'm a bit different now. *Todo cambia. Konke kuyashintsha.* Everything changes.

All of which leaves me wondering (if not wandering, not quite so much as Odysseus), which I would prefer, of the two options that Odysseus and his sailors undergo: one is the protection of the gods, with sex and magic. The other is a painful process of becoming yourself again, a slightly scrubbed-up version. Both, would be good; I'd like to do both. And as Odysseus comments, "the gods, after all, can do anything." But if that wasn't available, if you had to choose only one of those two options? Divine pleasures, or transformation but it's still always you. (Or maybe these are the same thing, after all.) Which is preferable, giving that we also factor in time, memory, language, substances, healing? We can think about this, ponder the literary, linguistic, mythical precursors. Maybe there's an option. Or in the end maybe it's not worth worrying about it; it's just fate toying with us like a bad orca prances around with the sad salmon. Or maybe it's like Odysseus says as he sets out from his ships, "I have absolutely no choice." I'll think about it. Unless I forget.

—

Thanks to Jack White and Olivia Mole.

Kat MEADS

Anatomy of a Scene

Canadian turned Parisian Mavis Gallant, renowned for her short fiction, also wrote two novels and a play. There were murmurs that she was working on a third novel at the time of her death in 2014, but we Gallant readers have only the two, the second, *A Fairly Good Time*, published in 1970. A tale of despondency, mettle and eccentricity as exhibited by two generations of women, the novel might have come off a complete downer in the hands of another author, but as delivered by Gallant, starting with the ironic title, it is as frequently funny—brutally funny—as it is sharply poignant.

Like her creator, protagonist Shirley (Norrington Higgins) Perrigny is a Canadian living in Paris, currently married to Phillipe, a journalist, who seems to have done a runner. Her first husband died on their honeymoon. She works as an interpreter (of sorts) in a department store, is terrified of her in-laws, keeps a messy house, reads compulsively, has very poor eyesight, saves a friend from suicide and from her mother in Canada receives letters describing bluebells and containing admonitions not "to cry whilst writing letters. The person receiving the letter is apt to take it as a reproach."

It is Shirley's mother who alerts her that Cat Castle, a woman "who has known you since before you were born" is also in Paris (as a tourist) and insists that Shirley "make an effort" to see her. There follows chapter three, composed of a single scene, wherein Shirley—or Shirl, as Mrs. Castle calls her—joins Mrs. Castle for Mrs. Castle's third breakfast of the morning at the Pons Tearoom, a recommended tourist destination. When Shirley admits she didn't realize the Pons Tearoom was "so famous," Mrs. Castle, in disbelief, snarks: "Let's hope it meets your standards." Far from offending Shirley, the "sarcasm made the old woman familiar; her voice might have risen out of this morning's letter," penned by Shirley's mother.

By meeting up both women are doing their duty: Shirley, at her mother's behest; Mrs. Castle, as Shirley's mother's spy. Throughout the encounter, the generational divide is on full display. Mrs. Castle (as herself and as a stand-in for Shirley's mother) are exemplars of the "tough it out" school, women who have learned not to privilege emotional pain and disappointment as a special condition worthy of discussion. Shirley Perrigny, who continuously expresses distress and befuddlement, is another breed.

Gallant structures the scene as two characters talking past each other while simultaneously laying in much of Shirley's backstory and setting up a good chunk of what the reader can expect of Shirley, in terms of behavior, as the story continues and Mrs. Castle goes her own way.

Among the topics covered and situations disclosed: Shirley's mother's idiosyncrasies; Shirley's two marriages; her pregnancy during her second honeymoon; her current husband Phillipe's character and their marital relationship ("When we have a fight he never fights. He just listens and corrects my French sometimes and then he gives me a couple of phenobarb"); what her in-laws think of Shirley and she of them; Shirley's particular brand of deep observation coupled with absentmindedness; the occasional flare of expatriate homesickness (Mrs. Castle's "ugly prairie accent" brings "tears of pleasure" to Shirley's eyes).

Mrs. Castle, we learn, is no Henry Jamesian character, embracing the continent and its ways. Proudly and sternly she announces to the tea-room waitress: "We are from Canada," prepared to "turn the waitress to stone should she attempt to deny it." Mrs. Castle has undertaken the European tour "in order to show her children back in Canada she did not need them" and takes notes she intends to record so that her family "can spend a Sunday listening" to her trip details and she won't have to talk about it further. She thinks her sons have married "selfish little snobs" and her daughter Phyllis "hadn't done all that well either." She shows up at the tearoom in a "Salzburger cape and hat" and "butterfly spectacles" and armed with opinions—lots and lots of opinions.

The scene opens with Shirley's announcement that she's "just this second" remembered she's supposed to have lunch at Phillipe's mother's, assuring herself aloud that at his mother's house the missing, incommunicado Phillipe must be. We get our first hint of how Gallant will use Mrs. Castle in the scene when she bluntly responds to that husband-at-mother's reveal: "Bad place for a man."

Neither Shirley with her black coffee nor Mrs. Castle with her two eclairs stand on ceremony.

They talk about Shirley's mother, Margaret, who, according to Mrs. Castle, "doesn't believe in anything but reincarnation anymore," used to "stare down" Shirley's father when he tried to hold her hand in public, saying "'Teddy, don't be dirty,'" and currently suffers from cancer, Mrs. Castle believes, not "stomach flu." When Shirley admits that she has confessed to her mother that she "thought she was messing up (her) marriage,

doing all the wrong things," Mrs. Castle replies: "You shouldn't have mentioned that part about marriage." According to Mrs. Castle, Margaret wouldn't have appreciated hearing about that.

They talk about Shirley's friend Renata who needed an abortion that Shirley helped to arrange. "From the word go, Shirl, what did it have to do with you?" responds Mrs. Castle, blaming Shirley's heritage for her rescue tendencies. "Honest to God, any old bum your grandfather could pick up off the street he'd bring home."

When Shirley admits she hasn't told Phillipe about Renata but now thinks she'd "better tell him the truth before it gets any more complicated," Mrs. Castle responds: "No point. If you start on a long-winded story like you keep doing with me, he'll drop off to sleep . . . You don't have to go through life saying any daft-sounding thing just because it happens to be true. Keep it plausible but mostly keep it short."

In Shirley's next "long-winded" story, she details the sad state of her relationship to Phillipe, both living separate lives, Shirley attending parties on her own. "Even when he's here he won't go anywhere if it's a Saturday. But I think Saturday night is lonely just staying home. To tell you the truth, Philippe scares me." Shirley is also "scared" to go to her mother-in-law's, where she's "nervous all the time" and feels "judged for things I don't understand."

"Why are you always in such a hurry to get married, I wonder?" Mrs. Castle muses aloud. "You seem to get married in a rush, then you rush the other way." Initially (and silently) Shirley considers the "married in a rush" sentiment to hit "wide of the mark" because of the amount of paperwork that's "needed for the marriage of a French citizen to a foreigner." But then she pivots, answering: "I was in a rush to get married because I thought he was sent from heaven . . . I was twenty-five and all the men I knew were married or childish or neurotic or homosexual."

Mrs. Castle abruptly brings the breakfast to a close by gifting Shirley a passed-down religious tract she discovered when "doing out the house before coming over here." *The Peep of Day* came into Mrs. Castle's possession because Shirley's grandmother had "overlooked" her daughter

Margaret and given the pamphlet instead to Mrs. Castle, whom she considered her goddaughter. Mrs. Castle, correcting the error, adds an additional inscription: "For Shirley Norrington, souvenir of a meeting in Paris, this book comes back to by rights." Instantly Shirley starts reading.

When Shirley suggests they meet again, Mrs. Castle scotches the plan.

> "There's no real need, is there? I've had a good look at you and I know what to tell your mother. We've been here, at Pons, which I was desiring to see . . ."

> "What are you going to say to Mother?"

> "Nothing I couldn't put on tape for others to hear. That you're thin as a rail and you seem to know a lot of people. You're about like you always were, to tell you the truth. Reading instead of listening. Life isn't books. Did you know you were born feet first? If we see each other again sometime I'll tell you a lot that might interest you."

As Mrs. Castle heads off for her bus, Shirley remembers that she mistakenly left her apartment with no money. Might Mrs. Castle lend her a bit? She'll bring the repayment tomorrow to Mrs. Castle's hotel.

The chapter's final lines belong to Mrs. Castle, Mrs. Castle's "prairie voice" and Mrs. Castle's credo.

> "Now, that's something I'd just never do . . . You've had your book, and you've had your breakfast, and that's all I'm good for. Anyway, Shirl, your mother would be the first to remind you that a lady never needs anything. Never needs, never wants. Anyway, never asks."

Anyway, never asks.
Crackerjack finish to a crackerjack scene.

Sonya Moor

Another writer: Pö

Go back twenty odd years and my *quartier* told a different story. Before the mushrooming of yoga studios, vintage eateries, concept stores and online-only supermarkets, Paris's eleventh arrondissement festered with disaffected workshops. Skeletons of cracking timber and desquamating walls in tones of rancid butter, school-house brown, and utility blue-lead paint— huddled around courtyards caving into the cellars below. These were screened by immense coach doors made immovable by their own decay. Here and there, the industrial rooftops of abandoned factories took jagged bites out of the skyline. Artists scrambled to claim cheap metres squared, while squatters found abundant lodgings for less. Cats were pest control. Dogs were security.

A few aging cabinetmakers, upholsterers and furniture painters remained—traces of the furniture industry that once flourished on the rue du Faubourg Saint-Antoine. Straw and stuffing clogged the drains outside their workshops. Gutters ran with rainbows from industrial dyes tipped directly into the streets, making archipelagos of the dog dirt.

There was graffiti everywhere.

Everywhere.

Walls boasted art that was not yet fully recognised as such: Miss.Tic's sassy stencils, Jérôme Mesnager's shadowy silhouettes, Kraken's tentacles, or eL Seed's arabesques . . . And great seething pile-ups of tags.

One reappeared with particular regularity: Pö. More often: PöPö. Or even: PöPöPö. Sometimes with crew names. But always Pö on top, biggest and most visible.

Pö got places where the getting required guts and imagination—also ropes, ladders and close, protective clothing. It was necessarily an exercise in mountaineering, a parkour of attic traps, lead piping, rusting rungs up chimney stacks, and finger-tip, toe-hold ledges. Even from lower rooftops, a fall onto unforgiving cobbles could turn a skull to melon skin. As for the zinc heights, with their bright-day glare and grey-day menace to good grip, why would anyone go there?

Testosterone, I figured.

Pö's signature text-speak interrupted passers-by, with urgent demands—often the kind that skirt wearers could expect to be subjected to in the street.

Il fo vraiment ke je tir un cou—*Il faut vraiment que je tire un coup*—I really need to fuck

Je sui tro en chien frer—*Je suis trop en chien, frère*—I gotta get a fuck/fix, bro

J'ai tro la dal—*J'ai trop la dale*—I'm crazy hungry [for food, sex . . .]

The words were incomprehensible until spoken, at least silently. As they claimed mind-space and breath, readers voiced lascivious appetites and suffered their imposition. The gender agreements are inconsistent, further troubling the notion of who, exactly, was voicing and being voiced.

In the same stroke, Pö's pigments put people in a place that should have felt safe. With brushes and rollers wielded from the end of broom handles or some such, Pö repainted the grubby onzième in nursery colours: baby blue, toothpaste white, bubblegum pink and duckling yellow.

Passing a wall pot-bellied with tags, or a newly defaced shopfront, people tutted, 'Dogs pissing play the same game.'

With Pö, though, the game was uncertain.

Shifty multiple meanings and strikeouts evidenced word play, for sure. But the signs suggested not so much a laying claim as a veiled reveal or disruption:

PöPö NiK ~~Tou~~-Pas—*PöPö nique ~~tout~~ pas*—PöPö fuck(s) everything/PöPö doesn't fuck

Paris's police force boasts a dedicated anti-tag brigade that works full time, building files on offenders, who risk punishments proportional to surface area of damage, with prison sentences up to two years and fines up to €30,000. In a video available online, a member of the anti-tag brigade explains her mission: 'Nobody feels safe in spaces covered in graffiti.'

When working a *punition*—punishment (the schoolroom word-theft used to describe multiple tags by the same tagger), Pö's 'p' sometimes formed a head and tail. The effect was a public discharge of monstrous spermatozoa.

But Pö's style was also disarmingly girly. Love hearts replaced o's, and dotted j's and i's, bringing to mind messages covertly swapped at the back of classrooms, etched beneath desk lids, or slicked across tiles in toilet cubicles.

Some of Pö's street messages spoke the loneliness of the city, and reached out across it:

Cé our kan on est seul—*C'est au cas où on est seul*—This is in case we're alone

Others repurposed public space to convey one-to-one communications:

Au ca ou jarriv pa a te fer un calin je te fai un grafiti bon voyage manon—

Au cas où je n'arrive pas à te faire un câlin, je te fais un graffiti: bon voyage Manon—

In case I don't manage to give you a hug, I'm doing a graffiti: happy travels, Manon

Pö was frequently tagged after the word *signé*—signed, for extra insistence. But Pö's work defied the space-grab-turf-mark approach, with humour and startling vulnerability. One work consisted of rude words that were both big—metres squared of yelling caps—and clever, with the repeated a's flinging the swear-word string into a one-word epic:

AAAAAAAAAAAAAAAAABîtecuchatteputepute Pö—

AAAAAAAAAAAAAAAAABîteculchatteputepute Pö—

AAAAAAAAAAAAAAAAACockarsecuntfuckfuck Pö

Others came accompanied by the story of their making: pentimenti and critical self-assessments.

Bra = tou pété—*Le bras est tout pété*—I messed up doing the arm

À la base c'est ici que je voulais le faire—To start with I wanted to do it [the graffiti] here [indicated by an arrow]

Or engaged in almost kinky self-exposure.

J'ai dé poile sur le téton—*J'ai des poils sur le téton*—I've got hairy nipples

Or suggested a more profound working through—the kind normally done on a therapist's couch.

Je suis nul en séduction—I'm crap when it comes to seduction

J'ai peur de filles—Girls scare me

Un jour je serai sexi—One day I'll be sexy

While approaches varied, the theme was constant—Pö's graffiti spelt it out: **L'amour et le**

sexe—Love and sex. Repeated over and over, like a trauma.

Given the danger of prosecution, anonymity is commonly seen as both source and cost of a tagger's freedom of expression. But the extreme intimacy of Pö's declarations raised deeper questions of what *essentially* belongs to each person: while walls are fair game, privacy preserves what should be an inviolable personal space.

In a self-assumed public-and-most-private space, Pö said the unsayable.

J'ai casimen jamais fai l'amour—*J'ai quasiment jamais fait l'amour*—I've practically never made love

J'aimerais bien fair l'amour—*J'aimerais bien faire l'amour*—I'd really like to make love/I'd like to make love properly

A graffiti aficionado clued me to a better-adjusted reading of Pö's work.

'I love the complexity of his word play.' I declared.

'You know it's Pö,' she responded, 'As in Pauline?'

A female, then.

Who goes by a diminutive.

Written BIG.

Pö's shouts to be heard and her space transgressions took on altered significance—as did her anonymity.

A picture: In what looks like a disaffected railway station, the artist stands upfront, in a *wesh* uniform of baggy tracky-b's, t-shirt and denim jacket, face covered by a mask: the Teletubby Po. Feet wide, broom handle tilted, here is a dandy king with a curious sceptre. In the background are words bigger than mansize: **PöPö NiK ~~Tou~~ Pas**

Now, Pö is also known as Pauline Conforti, artist.

The blurb for her first solo exhibition made it clear that 'artist' was a role she did not feel comfortable claiming; she hesitated to describe her work as 'contemporary art', but felt she could not very well describe it any other way. This after ten years of illustrious graffiti.

Her participative exhibition, entitled *Je t'aime Papa*, explored through installations, texts and paintings her memories of incest. Despite the violence of the theme, she attempted an approach through humour, provocation and poetry.

Five years later, Pauline Conforti presented a school-fête inspired participative exhibition, themed around surfing life's ups and downs with optimism, marking distance from previous works treating 'darker subject matter'. The blurb made clear that one thing had not changed: reticence to claim the role of 'artist' and assume the description of 'contemporary art' for her work— but again, she felt she could not very well describe it any other way. By then, Conforti was a Beaux Arts graduate.

Walking, the other day by a church in what used to be a no-go area, I spotted Pö's cheeky-bum character newly tagged on a corner of what was once a squat and is now a boho-chic apartment block. Opposite the tagged wall was once a churchyard alley, where I suffered an assault. The alley has since been reclaimed by the city from the church, which itself was recently restored. Inside the chapel, a previously greige fresco sunbursts gold into lapis skies. The church's only other claim to cultural glory, the grave of a maybe-royal child, victim of the revolution, has been demoted to the grave of a commoner.

The alley is now integrated into a caged sports pitch, used primarily by inhabitants of the increasingly incongruous social-housing blocks. Young men grown too fast into broad chests and biceps animate the space, pounding tarmac with basketballs. On the other side of the church is a new kid's play area. Across the way is a small ornamental garden, edged with benches—mostly empty. The square is not unsafe, now, but the lack of footfall suggests I am not the only local who, when passing, still runs a mental risk assessment. Or opts for a detour, when time allows.

The sight of Pö's tag incited a mental meander, summoning to mind the story I heard about Pö's cheeky-bum character. According to the aficionado who said it was 'Pö' as in 'Pauline', when visiting Berlin, Pö discovered that her tag, voiced in German, was a homophone for 'butt'. Rather than let her tag be devalorised by word-association, the artist acknowledged, appropriated,

14

and subversively gloried in it, integrating it into her artistic vocabulary.

Similarly, Pö's cheeky-bum seems to at once acknowledge and unsettle present and previous claims upon the square. The place is surely no better frequented since Pö's tag was written into it, and I could not testify to the anti-tag brigade that Pö's graffiti makes me feel safe there—or even safer. But heartened, perhaps, yes. Her work's irreverence and joy seem to reach beyond the limits of the spray-can scrawl to rewrite inner landscapes, changing the way the site is perceived and experienced.

Eventually, the combined forces of the Mairie and the anti-tag brigade will blast Pö's tag to oblivion. It is only a matter of time. But—for at least a while after—the newly cleaned brickwork will speak the tag's absence, restoring it. Passers-by such as myself will keep returning the tag to the site, in memory. There it will be—and not be. Like the alley that once was, and is now haunted by yells from a basketball court. And the sleeping boy who is, and is not, a prince. Pö's cheeky-bum character both recognises and undermines these voices, mooning at them. Her work talks back, speaks out of turn, brings down to size even the most vociferous claims to the site. Her work prises open the past's tenacious hold over the present, without itself claiming dominance. Where Pö leaves her mark, she makes space—for something else to happen.

Shifra Sharlin

Publishing Is Murder

A True Crime Book Review

Not long ago, *The Washington Post* published an article under the headline: "Author of children's book on grief to stand trial for husband's murder." A Utah woman, Kouri Richens, allegedly murdered her husband and then wrote a book on grief for her children. A former Salt Lake County prosecutor, Curtis Tuttle speculated that the prosecution would attempt to enter the book as evidence in order to show that she is "callous." Mr. Tuttle concluded: "It's not a great look for her."

Mr. Tuttle travels in the wrong circles.

We writers get it: publishing is murder. The prosecution intends to argue that Kouri Richens acted out of the classic motives: sex and money. But any writer could tell you her true motive: getting published.

What don't writers do to publish a book in this era of publishing consolidation—the big five are now the big three and still more consolidation threatens, small presses belong to big presses, and as if that's not bad enough nobody is buying books. Established writers, writers whose books have won national recognition, writers with international reputations scramble to find a publisher. What won't they do to place a book? They collect blurbs, they get new agents, go to lunch, go to conferences, call up old friends, call in favors. Is it any wonder that the aspiring, unpublished writer would be driven to homicide?

Some have alleged that Mrs. Richins made many mistakes in committing murder. Did she really bungle her husband's murder at least twice? What really happened on that Greek vacation or, later, on Valentine's Day when she allegedly poisoned the husband's sandwich before her tryst with her lover? The intended victim allegedly alerted both friends and family: should he die, suspect his wife. His suspicions might have been the reason he was prompted to alter his will and his insurance policy so that, should she succeed, finally, in murdering him she would not collect the millions that could have paid off her killer debt (allegedly $5 million) but only what he had on his person (allegedly $25,00) and the stash in the home safe (allegedly $200,000). Those do look like serious errors in judgment, but Mrs. Richins got one thing right: grief is hot.

How hot? Never mind statistics or the fact that typing "grief" into the Amazon search window will turn up a dozen books published in the last ten years, which does not include all the books on grief that do not have grief in the title (Two bestsellers come to mind—Joan Didion's *The Year of Magical Thinking* and Kathryn Schulz's *Lost and Found*.) Forget that the proliferation of books on grief in every genre—poetry (this year's winner of *The Georgia Re-*

view's poetry prize is working on a "phenomenon-logy of embodied grief and loss"), fiction, memoir, and self-help. The quick and easy success of her book for children on grief confirms the astuteness of Mrs. Richins' calculation.

She racked up five-star reviews on Goodreads. Like Joan Didion's *Year of Magical Thinking*, Kouri Richins' *Are You With Me?* was praised on Goodreads for being both "heartbreaking" and "helpful." She secured interviews on local news and radio stations. After only one homicide, Kouri Richins had achieved every aspiring writer's dream: she was an established writer.

She saw a future for herself: sequels to her first book—one about a girl grieving her mother, another for siblings. It could have been big if only she had not been arrested for murder.

In an instant, her Goodreads ratings plunged from five stars to one. (Save for one three-star reviewer who hoped that the book would eventually emerge from under the cloud of the author's arrest for murder to be appreciated for the worthy book it is.) The sympathetic interviewers turned snarky. In short, she faced the condescension and accusations that many writers get, albeit not from criminal prosecutors. What writer has not been accused of exploiting their near and dear for material? The court of public opinion had reached a verdict: Kouri Richins had profited from her husband's death by writing about it.

And as writers have always had to do, Mrs. Richins has persisted in the face of negative reviews. In prison she has continued to write. In addition to the six-page letter to her mother headed with the exhortation to "Walk the Dog" and advising how her brother should testify, she has also written 60 pages of fiction.

Perhaps Mrs. Richins suffers from hypergraphia, a compulsion to write accompanied by the compulsion to research, often accompanied by epileptic seizures. Some argue that Dostoevsky suffered from this affliction. We'll never know whether or to what extent Kouri Richins is so afflicted. The digital forensic expert, who found the deleted texts between Mrs. Richins and her lover exchanged while Mr. Richins was dying from drinking a Moscow Mule cocktail

spiked with five times the lethal dose of fentanyl, did not attempt to recover Word files.

Had the expert looked, would they have found evidence of Mrs. Richins' longstanding efforts to hit upon a publishable topic? Maybe there's a draft of *Are You With Me?* about a husband who neglects his wife for big game hunting and his motorized vehicles, about a husband who owned, as Eric Richins did, "every motorized toy known to man" as his online obituary had it, a man who was known for his "calls to tell you he rolled the four-wheeler for the umpteenth time, is stuck, and needs you to come get him," a man whose contribution to home décor consisted of the heads of the big game he had hunted. But Mrs. Richins seems to have known her market. Nobody in Kamus, Utah would have been sympathetic to such a book.

Which brings me to another theory of the case. What if Mrs. Richins' bungled attempts at homicide were intentionally bungled? What if these bungled homicides were her cry for help? What if she had already tried more conventional means of asking her husband to, for instance, stop rolling his four-wheeler or going on big game hunts? What if she had seen the same movies and tv shows I have in which only drug dealers and bank robbers keep large sums of cash on their persons or in their home safes? If her husband had figured out that she was trying to kill him; did he ever ask himself why? Instead of going to her to clear up the matter, he went to his friends and to his sister. He changed his will and his life insurance, not his ways.

Not that I'm suggesting that murder is ever, under any circumstances a valid response to domestic, or other, complaints, nor am I blaming the victim. Killing people is wrong even if your motive was saving your marriage, a motive that, even her most ardent defenders, have not put forward. As a marriage-saving strategy, murder is a textbook case of self-sabotage. It's far more likely that Kouri Richins was trying to get material for her book.

But did she have to go so far as to pen an unconditionally loving dedication to the husband she allegedly murdered? Was such blatant hypocrisy necessary? Former Utah prosecutor Tuttle surely would have seen Mrs. Richins' bad enough look getting even worse. In this, too, he shows no understanding of the demanding craft of writing and no appreciation of the fearsomeness of Mrs. Richins' commitment to publishing. There are structural constraints. The grief genre is not for sissies.

In every occasion, in every genre, there are some things you can say and some things you cannot. At funerals and in books on grief, nobody talks about the somewhat dearly departed. With that questionable dedication Kouri Richins demonstrated her own dedication to her book project.

And, to be honest, Mrs. Richins was not the only one with a publishing motive. Could Eric Richins have been planning to fake his death—with his wife's assistance—in order to create the conditions for her book? What about Eric Richins' friends and family? Perhaps his sister had a scheme to publish a book on sibling grief? Somebody must have thought of the self-help angle. Those books always sell. Not the homicide part, but the what-to-say-to-the-grief-stricken part. Who's to say that a neighbor is not, even now, penning just such a much-needed volume. Or what about a prosecutor with an eye on the market for hot takes on bad looks for accused murderers. When it's murder to publish, you can always make a killing.

Postscript: Since the author's arrest, *Are You With Me?* is no longer available on Amazon. Rumor has it that a copy is available on ebay for about $900. A video of the book being read aloud, made before the arrest, was still available on youtube when this reviewer last checked.

Lawrence Winkler

Panama Pirate

'Now and then we had a hope that if we lived and were good, God would permit us to be pirates.'

Mark Twain, *Life on the Mississippi*

After a downpour and some green guayabas off a roadside tree, I hitch-hiked all the way to Panama City and the very inexpensive Pension Nacional. I asked for a room.

"Por hora o por la noche?" the Hairy Beast behind the desk inquired. *By the hour or by the night.* I should have looked elsewhere. After I returned from a pizza and a *Panama* beer, my equilibrium was disrupted hourly by the rotating musical bed frames shuddering in quadraphonic surround sound through the walls. My own bed bounced in counterpoint with the adjacent neighbors and the cycles of moaning in the humid heat, mosquitoes and acrid rancidity almost drove me mad. When daylight finally came, I checked out hurriedly for a breakfast of fried platanos, but I really felt like a cigarette.

Panama owes its existence to piracy and mosquitoes. The conquistadors robbed land and labor from 200,000 original indigenous villagers, to haul stolen gold and silver from South America, across the isthmus, for shipment to Spain. English, Dutch, and French pirates (and escaped black slave *Cimarrons*) seized treasure from the Spaniards. Teddy Roosevelt eventually expropriated the whole country, from Colombia. But the mosquitoes stole blood and lives from everyone—in exchange for Yellow Fever and Malaria. The original Spanish route across the isthmus was called the *Camino de Cruces,* the Road of the Crosses. For a reason. Scotland is not independent today because more than half the wealth of the country in 1700 had been ploughed into a failed scheme to colonize the Darien. When the mosquitoes won, Scotland was forced to seek a union with England. The French attempt to build a canal in 1880 failed because they lost 22,000 men to disease unwittingly concentrated in the unscreened hospital wards they had also poorly constructed. It took Walter Reed to finally prove the 'Mosquito hypothesis,' and Teddy took it to the bank. The Panama Canal opened for business in 1914.

And that ultimately left me standing, anesthetized by sugar and suburbia, on this American Graffiti backdrop. I had come to the Canal Zone because I used to collect the postage stamps. They were so 'clean,' particularly beside the República Panama stamps, on the adjacent page in my album. And so it was in real life. I was eating a Baskin Robbins ice cream cone and, despite my Herculean three-month effort, hitchhiking farther and further into what I thought was the heart of Latin America, I had emerged in Smallville. The receiving townspeople were aptly called 'Zonians.' Live long and prosper. They were playing *Happy Days* in the reality refugee soda shop, and I'm pretty sure it was Norman Rockwell himself who dug down that extra knuckle to get me a supersized scoop of Rocky Road. My first experience with culture shock was ironically destined to be with my own culture. For the second time that day, I felt like a cigarette. Instead, I bought a watch, and a bus ticket to Colon. I was going to be a pirate.

I was ambivalent about Colon. The emphasis was on the last syllable, although you could be forgiven for thinking otherwise. It started as an island swamp of dense mangrove, poisonous manzanillo trees, stinging insects, venomous snakes, alligators, and unhealthy marsh vapor, hanging over heavy ooze. Then the Americans came in and ruined it. It was the Atlantic terminus of the Panama railroad, built to transport Eastern seaboard would-be miners to the California gold rush. During its heyday it had some cachet, but the Colombians burned it down in 1885. The Panamanians did it again in 1915, and political riots finished it off in the 1960s. By the time I got there, in 1980, it was a poor and dangerous place. There were two-storied wooden buildings with overhanging upper floor balcony balustrades, street-level drinking holes with swinging doors, and drug dealers and prostitutes, leaning along narrow filthy walls. Colon was different from Belize City though. In Colon, even the townspeople were afraid. I went right for the boats moored on the contraband docks, down Calle Cinco. Here were dozens of small rust-bucket cargo ships, smuggling electronics, textiles, cigarettes, and liquor, into the Colombian Guajira, and bringing back goodness-knows-what. I had a name, from Hairy Beast at the Hotel Nacional in Panama City. It wasn't hard to find him. Or his boat, the *Cha Chi*. It was already loaded to the rafters with contraband.

"You're a doctor?" asked Captain Lemos. I answered in the affirmative.

He was having some comprehension difficulty.

"Look." I said. "I'm a doctor in my other life, but in this one, I'm a pirate." He asked me why I really wanted to join his crew. I told him I had an aversion to flying. He shrugged.

"You'll have to work as hard as the other men." I looked around at the other men. They were cooking on propane stoves, drinking rum, and dozing in their hammocks. Young girls in red and pink hot pants, showing far too much cleavage, were hanging around the gangplank. I told him I could handle it.

He informed me that the *Cha Chi* would likely sail the next day before noon, and that I should report at dawn. We shook on it.

Back in the 'hood, I met the razor sharp 87-year-old Guatemalan dueña of the Pension Acropolis and signed in my occupation as '*pirata*.' Despite the raised eyebrow, she gave me a quiet room, with a double bed, ceiling fan, sink, dresser, and a spotless WC (without the seat, of course). I had a cold shower and went shopping. I found an Olympus XA camera, for the same price I had paid in Seattle, and christened it 'Oracle II.' The dueña had suggested Café Panama for a good cheap evening meal. The place was hot, crowded, and smoky, and I had trouble hearing the Chinese proprietor take my order over the constant crash of cutlery and plates, on wood and on each other. I had the *bistek*. For me it was cheap. For the patron who strolled up to the counter next to me, it was apparently free. He was a big black guy, wearing sunglasses and his body weight in bling, and he had a cocked pistol in the holster hanging over his right shoulder. The owner didn't take his order and never made eye contact with him, but a big plate of meat and manioc floated down beside me. The gangsta rocked like he was listening to some inner Marley, and his elbows flapped and mapped his territory. He ate fast, using his fork as a shovel and, with a flourish of his left forearm, wiped his mouth, and left the cafeteria, no tip, and fear and loathing in Chinese eyes.

I left the pension at dawn the next morning, and not a moment before. When I reached the

Cha Chi, everyone, including Captain Lemos, was still asleep. When I reported for duty, he asked me why I was there so early. I reminded him of our conversation the day before, but he obviously wasn't a stickler for details. The other item he forgot to mention was that he had lied about when they were going to Colombia. He said he didn't really know. I asked him if there was another Captain who did know. He pointed down the pier to an eighty-foot double-decked white ship, with a low wheelhouse, tall signal mast, twin funnels and crane. It said *Rina II* on the bow. I said goodbye to Captain Lemos, and hello to Captain Garcia. We hit it off immediately and he introduced me to the crew. There was Nicholas, a young bright Colombian deckhand, full of vinegar. He played a mean game of magnetic chess. Manga was the quiet but deep muscular local boy made good. He and his simple paisano, Milton, were the cargo-shifting workhorses of the *Rina II*. Francisco was a chubby, quite older marinero, and the mechanic was an old practical joker, named Eduardo. He was always sneaking rubber spiders and snakes into your hammock, the latrine, or your food, or showing off by chewing fish bones. But he could also be moody, especially after a little rum. Pedro was the macho cook. If you didn't like it, you wouldn't get as much next time. Every meal was some kind of meat stew with manioc or plantain. One day he made a salad, to the surprise of the crew. That was the last time. Other occasional visitors were always coming and going. There was Luis, a chemist from Costa Rica, William, a 'Hey Mon' Colombian and his friend, also named Eduardo, and girlfriends too numerous to count. The real boat people were a French couple, Guy and Madeleine, who were trying to travel to Colombia with one pack, a guitar, roll-your-own tobacco, and high hopes. She was six months pregnant. The crew was nervous and puzzled by their priorities, and, admittedly, so was I.

The next five days and nights aboard the *Rina II* are now remote fond memories. I worked hard, loading the ship with televisions under the watchful gaze of the mafia owners, but there was also plenty of hammock time, for reading, crossword puzzles, and playing magnetic chess with the crew. These men were true coconuts—hard as nails, sweet inside. Milton and I went out for a beer one night and met Gloria of the Vibrating Hips. On another afternoon, I got a fishbone stuck in my throat, and I wasn't even trying to emulate Eduardo. Every morning, we were leaving tomorrow. *Mañana*.

The fifth day, for a change, I left the boat and took a bus to Portobelo. The remains of the half-moon black shantytown and its Spanish forts were deceivingly ordinary. In its day, the 'beautiful port' was one of the most important settlements on the Spanish Main. Columbus named it in 1502, for the refuge it provided from a terrible storm but, until there was a good reason to live there, there was no good reason to live there. It rained every day. Decay was, and still is, heavy in the air. The jungle grew as fast as machetes could cut it down. But what gold was to Colon, silver was to Portobelo. The Spaniards brought so much silver from here so fast, that the value of the metal fell so far, that Mediterranean economies faltered. Taxes rose to keep up with the resulting inflation, and Middle Eastern rulers suddenly needed credit from Europe. Real bad. The Ottoman Empire collapsed from within, and external colonization prepared the way for the eventual creation of today's nation-states.

I stood on the parapets of the 'Castle of Iron,' *El Castillo de San Felipe de Todo Fierro*. It wasn't iron that the strength of the fort derived from, however. It was coral. The reefs were easily mined underwater, when it was still soft. It dried so strong that the fort's three-meter walls were impervious to cannonballs. It was like a giant mattress that only strengthened with each impact dent. In 1739, British Admiral Edward Vernon (for which George Washington's estate in Virginia was named), despite capturing the town, gave up trying to blow up the fortifications, after 18 days of futile effort. He was there because of 'Spanish Depredations upon the British Subjects', and particularly the War of Jenkin's Ear. In 1731 Robert Jenkins, captain of the British brig *Rebecca*, met Julio León Fandiño, captain of the Spanish coast guard vessel, *La Isabela*. It wasn't a cordial exchange. Fandiño had boarded Jenkin's ship and cut off his left ear. Because he was a pirate.

And that was the real reason I was standing on the battlements of the Iron Castle, peering out into the bay. I was looking at the burial site of Sir Francis Drake, dropped into the water in a lead coffin, after he died of 'bloody flux' dysentery aboard his ship, *Defiance*, in 1596.

Portobelo had been a pirate playground. Their history began, in a less than noble fashion, with marooned or escaped English, French or Dutch seamen, on the northwest corner of the island of Española, now Haiti. They survived by hunting feral pigs and cattle with dogs and cutlasses. The meat was smoked on a 'barbacoa,' to preserve it. The natives called the jerky 'bucan,' and the Spanish eventually started hunting down the animals the 'buccaneers' were dependent on, after they began trading their meat with pirates. The Spaniards were so successful that the buccaneers had to turn to hunting galleons instead. *You can have too much of a good thing.* The French called them 'flibustier,' and the English called the French 'filibusters.' It didn't really matter. In the end, buccaneers, filibusters, and pirates were all the same savage.

Two savages were associated with Portbelo. The first was Henry Morgan, who captured the town in 1668, with a fleet of privateers and 450 men. The scale of his brutality, murder, torture, and rape, was unprecedented. He plundered the place bare for two weeks. The second was François l'Olonnais, who was even worse. He attacked and robbed the coastal Indians all other pirates depended on. He once beheaded 70 Spaniards with his sword, and sent the heads to the Governor of Nombre de Dios, piled high in a native canoe. On another occasion he cut out the heart of a young woman, ate it while it was still beating, and reportedly washed it down with a cup of her blood. But you knew it wasn't going to last. A year before Morgan sacked Portobelo, l'Ollonois attacked the wrong galleon leaving the bay. It was loaded with veteran soldiers, and he only managed to escape to the Darien coast, where he once again threatened the Indians who had come to his assistance. They put his pieces on a roasting spit and ate him.

'Ah, Miss Purity, 'tis good to be back in Portobelo.' I could hear Robert Newton's West Country accent as I reached down for the shiny thing in an obscure corner of the fort wall. It was a piece of eight long john sliver. *Arrrgh, matey. Thar be a bit o' treasure.*

I walked up through the hills above Portobelo and examined some of the small 'casamata' forts, where the Spaniards had stored gunpowder and arms. The view of the quiet bay was spectacular. A small boy passed me on horseback as I made my sweaty descent.

When I got back to the *Rina II*, Captain Garcia was waiting to talk to me. The Colombians had raided two contraband boats right out of the water, while I was gone. The mafia was spooked enough that we wouldn't be going to the Guajira for at least a fortnight. I thanked him and resorted to my least desirable option.

I really didn't want to fly into South America. It was unromantic and ignoble. But I also didn't want to travel overland through the Darien Gap. There were good reasons why it was the missing link on the Pan American highway. At that time, there were no marked trails through a hundred miles of impenetrable swamps and jungle. The biodiversity was not your friend. And the human wildlife consisted of FARC guerillas, drug traffickers, kidnappers, and paranoid paramilitaries. None of this really bothered me. I just suddenly felt the need for speed.

I said goodbye to the crew next morning and took a bus to Panama City, and another to Tucumen airport. I bought the cheapest ticket I could to a continent shaped like my farewell cake three months earlier. I'd never heard of the destination, but it was printed in bold letters on my boarding pass. **Medellín.**

Aug Stone

Count In

He claimed to be the Comte de Saint Germain, though I'm really not sure this was true. I first became aware of his presence when I was standing in the queue at The Reality Café, my local coffee shop, and overheard him ask the cashier "What exactly do you mean by 'soy milk'?" He walked away with an empty cup. I thought no more about it until he sidled up to me while I was trying to enjoy my own beverage in this precious break from work—an auditor for a percussionists' guild if you must know, believe me I've heard the "you don't miss a beat" jokes more times than you can shake a stick at—and this stranger began to regale me with all manner of stories. Which, to be fair, given the range of millennia, would be proof he was who he claimed. Though something didn't quite sit right . . .

"I was there, you know, when Pope John XXIII started his Jimi Hendrix Experience cover band. Dude didn't even play guitar, just carried a surfboard around and pointed to different sections of the deck while a friend of his, wrapped in bandages from head to toe so of course rumors abounded it was a different guy each time, well this someone threw tennis balls at a cage of parrots. The birds weren't even trained to squawk a single word, certainly not any of Hendrix's lyrics, and there wasn't a purple feather in sight to tie the whole spectacle together. It's like that time I caught Stravinsky trying to charge his mobile phone at a whack-a-mole kiosk, at least I thought it was Stravinsky, though certain sycophants will assert they never saw him puttering about in a sky blue astronaut helmet and matching yoga pants, no shirt on to boot. But you gotta be a little bit out there to make that kind of music. Heard he sent the first ever fax too, the lyrics of Mind Riot to Chris Cornell, wasn't even concerned about royalties, had made enough already, and that's why he's not credited on the *Badmotorfinger* album. The best was hanging out with Dickens though. Imagine if that guy had access to a fax machine. Killed so many carrier pigeons sending last minute revisions to his publisher, weighed those birds down good. But that really takes me back, cause people don't know it, I mean sure they all oo and ah 'DaVinci was the one who invented the helicopter', though they never talk about his heli-PAD! That thing was hoppin'! DJs playin' deep house, a hottub in each corner, street vendors selling candied hawks' wings for a buck a pop! Wash 'em down with a pineapple milkshake, none of that soy malarkey they were tryin' to gouge me for, but the delicious milk of the emu. Ol' Leonardo would import them from Australia, couldn't get enough of 'em, had a steady stream arriving by boat almost weekly. Yeah, yeah, I know, you're not the first person to make the joke we were already on a helipad, and they could've been coptered in, what with their being flightless birds and all. But they'd be running around the landing, I mean this thing was huge, and DaVinci would pay buskers good money to chase after and try to milk them, all so he didn't have to hear another acoustic rendition of The Smiths' There Is A Light That Never Goes Out. He loved the song of course but Edison wouldn't shut up about it, giving those fellas a quarter an encore. Scene got a bit too intense after a while so I skedaddled over to Shanghai, desperately needed a haircut, I did, and was informed they had the best barber shop going. Little did I know the scamp who told me that meant quartet. I got roped into singing Goodnight Ladies more times than Teddy Vortdemere's had TV dinners—hot or cold. All because the banks weren't open when I arrived and there I was holding none of the local currency. Came back looking dandy, though. Nectarine keen. Was later told my arrival in LA that summer, strolling along the pier with Orson Welles, was what inspired The Little Old Lady From Pasadena. I was in drag to avoid the customs officers, obviously, smuggling in as I was enough China White to choke a horse. Not that that was what I intended to do with it. Heck, I ended up flushing the whole load down the toilet of an In N Out Burger when I realized I wasn't going to jail. One often takes on such escapades just for the thrill. Alright, you caught me. I did it because the tsarina bet me I couldn't. Never let it be said the ol' Comte de S. G. has been bested by Russian royalty. Sure, I knew Rasputin. Toured with Boney M too. And one night we were racing down the M2, Mötley Crüe were in town and we were all on our way to a Joy Division gig, when out of nowhere Mick Mars says to me he forgot his stage clothes back in a Denny's restroom in Kansas City. I said, Mick, those are long gone . You know Missouri loves company theatre. Put me in mind of my good buddy Harold Clitus, who everyone always mistakes for the real life Greek philosopher, knew him as well, but actually this H.C. was a tennis champion in Eastern Rumelia before that province was swallowed up by its Bulgarian neighbors. Not so much the tennis you or I would be familiar with today, more like a demented version of lawn darts played using live ammunition. Who knows? Maybe that's all the philosophy one ever needs. Like I told George III when I was trying to get him to change his name, worked a treat for Engelbert Humperdinck. Might've altered the course of history if he'd focused on having a career as a pop singer. You rarely get that in the monarchy, I even said so at the time. Oh but don't make me all maudlin. Reminds me of a brisk afternoon mid-construction on the Great Wall of China, I took my lunchbreak and sat at the edge with a fellow named Dumpty. You just don't get portents like that nowadays. Was many a year before I could bring myself to go back, and I still have vertigo thinking about it, the haircut debacle didn't help matters, but no way was I gonna miss a single show on that 1985 Wham! tour. I mean yeah there are those who say Magellan left so early cause he was hoping to arrive in time for the first concert, and Marco Polo was sent to inspect the indoor swimming pools they'd had on their rider. Makes sense. Who am I to cast doubts on how the music biz works? Back then you really had to put in the man hours to break an act. Believe me, DaVinci was planning to fly all the bands to him, as traveling by copter would've still been a novelty in his day. The issue being everyone wanted to do 'a quick pitstop' in Vienna to load up on cakes, pastries, and local confectionary, and always lost track of time. It's no coincidence so many of those early pop songs mention sugar, sweets, and candy. Yes, I am thinking of The Archies. Indubitably. I knew the real Jughead, was a Roman bowsman fond of the amphora. Given his military rank, he wouldn't dare

wear a crown. They'd have jugged his head, as he later told me when he saw the first issue of the comic. He wrote a memoir detailing his interactions with Asterix and Obelix and all those crazy Gauls, but insisted on penning it in Romansh so the book has only been brought out by a small Swiss press. Okay, you got me, CHapter is one of numerous companies I own. Nevertheless, I stand with my artists. The dough from Jug's foreign rights sales was tempting, let me tell you, though at the time I was understudying George Lazenby for that Bond film. And there are only so many hours in a day, my friend. Of course DaVinci was working on this too. You should've seen the clocks on that guy! Always looking for the Chuck D to his Flavor Flav. And if we're taking it back to the Swiss, what you've heard about the carnage at the 1850 yodeling competition in Bangkok is completely true. Naturally there were protests regarding the locale, but the food was superb. Breaks in the rioting to eat, scheduled in. And I guess yes, enough time has passed now I can confess my vocals were in fact on tape. Though I still say I deserve that third place medal as I was the only one bringing such technology to the table. After the market crash in '29 I did try to sell the award on eBay as it contained a fair amount of gold. Why don't I pen a memoir, I hear you ask? Especially with my Swiss publishing house, modest though it may be. And yes, of course, I need not follow dear Jughead's lead and confine myself to Romansh. Well, the idea is certainly enticing. Teddy Vortdemere has encouraged me on a number of occasions. Oh, the name doesn't ring a bell? Not that he wasted much energy on bells when it was all chimes and whistles. You really don't know him? Claimed you could pour linseed oil on a ghost and still get wet. What a flex! Took me to see his pal Baudelaire off on the Mayflower. I would later observe that poet embroiled in many a heated discussion with Frank Baum over bowls of noodles in various rundown backroom LA eateries. Ok, you got me again, I was the one serving said dishes. When you've lived as long as I have, you'll find it's mostly waiting. That *Wizard Of Oz* premiere in Wisconsin, woo boy, gave old Stravinsky a run for his money, spacecraft or not. No doubt you've read accounts of this? No? Pity. We've printed up a lovely little pamphlet with all the deets, called 'What's Left Of Spring?' Yes, the premiere was in August, what of it? I've learned of other WKRPs than were in Cincinnati. But I don't consider there to be any truth to the rumor that the Hamburglar was the real fifth Beatle and not George Martin. Or George Carlin. Stand-up back in the 1690s had outrageous jokes, really made you think. Had come a long way since Dante. Oh yes, I knew him too. Played tennis together. And proper tennis as well. Yes, yes, an infernal racket, you're with me now. He nixed that joke from the *Comedia* but kept it in his live set. The pyro was primitive back then though he was still well ahead of the curve. You've got to be, in those circles. They say Napolean used to watch bootleg films of some of those shows to relax after a tough day at the world domination game. You think Risk takes forever? You've no idea. Would I trade places with either of them? Not for all the peaches on Elba. Cuisine's more my line. The Comte de Compote they used to call me. Was quite germane. No, no, I'm not interested in going on any of those cooking programs that are omnipresent in our latest attempt at a millennia, assaulting the airwaves and the senses, except the ones most crucial to the outcome. A trivia show, perhaps. Having been here for a vast amount of history, that category is rather easy. But I tell ya, being friends with Ol' Van Winkle was hard work. I got into lifting weights in the interim and by the time he woke up, I was ripped. He's still groggy and I wanna go do an Iron Man, maybe catch a Black Sabbath gig afterwards. Plus there was so much explaining to do. Teddy Vortdemere had just invented a variation on duckpin bowling that Rip couldn't get his head around. We kept having to demonstrate it to him. Speaking of which, James Clerk Maxwell started off at a coffee house. At first he thought caffeine alone would give us perpetual motion."

And with that, my interlocutor disappeared out the doors of the Reality Café, quick as look-at-ya. As I am simply a denizen of the late 20th/early 21st centuries and can't prove otherwise, his claims to be the Comte seemed quite sound. But surely in all that time he'd have heard of soy milk?

Ron Ginzler

The Brezakian Symphony

Within the double-landlocked country of Uzbekistan (meaning one must travel through two other countries to reach any ocean) lies the world's only triple-landlocked country, the enclave known as Brezakia. Perched atop a forbidding plateau between the Aral and Caspian Seas—false seas, both are lakes, however salty they may be, and the Aral has almost dried up—Brezakia is not officially recognized as a country by Uzbekistan, or any other nation, which makes it impossible to find on maps.

The Brezakians, in turn, do not recognize Uzbekistan or any other nation and consider the world beyond their plateau a vast wilderness. Their land consists of a dozen scattered villages on their few dozen square miles of mostly arable land, their livelihood is from raising sheep and goats and an odd sort of inbred chicken which resembles the extinct dodo bird. They raise some vegetables of the leafy, grainy and tuberous kinds whose identity is not fully understood. They mine for metals and smelt them.

But their chief passion is music. All their instruments are unique to them, as are their scales. Every child learns to play and build every instrument as they learn to walk and talk.

The whole of the Brezakian people assemble twice a year on the solstices and play a vast symphony which lasts all night and through the next day, fortified by the strong quasi-barley-beer they brew. Numbering some five thousand, their number never increases due to high infant mortality, though it sometimes decreases.

There are no visitors to Brezakia. Even if one could climb the thousand foot cliffs that surround it, their language is so incomprehensible and their features so distinctive as to make disguise impossible, and they would instantly defenestrate a foreigner. The edge of their plateau forms their huge picture window on the outside world.

The discovery of the Brezakian Manuscript, as it was first known to the outside world, occurred on a June day in Uzbekistan. The sun was shining and white fleecy clouds like sheep marched obediently across the sky. A blue butterfly landed on the green moss that sat like a velvet cushion on the slate roof, then rose and merged with the sky.

The ancient manor house with its magnificent flying buttresses would have stood forever had the buttresses been made of stone as the rest of the edifice was, but termites had been busy and the front buttress, which terminated in a small studio atop a spiral staircase, abruptly collapsed, leading to the collapse of the larger building.

Under the termite-riddled floor boards of the studio was discovered a roll of parchment—actually a sheepskin—which a workman conveyed to the village schoolteacher.

The teacher took it to the University of K—, where for some years it sat in the office of the Chair of History, Professor Dmitry Eckzema, whose main virtue was maintaining his position after the collapse of the former Soviet Union.

After Eckzema's long-awaited death, the scroll was put in the rare-book room of the University Library, where a succession of doctoral students tried and failed to decipher it: it was written in no known language with no known alphabet. The librarian, fearing the incessant unrolling and rolling of the scroll by grubby fumbling graduate students would lead to its disintegration, photocopied it and sealed the original in the library's vault. He sent photocopies to half a dozen prominent scholars around the world.

Professor Jan van Jammer of Witwatersrand University claimed it a clever forgery from the late 19th century, but failed to mention what it was a forgery of, or why it was clever. He later revised his claim and said it was a hoax that meant nothing.

Dr. Rosetta Stone of Oxford (Magdelene College) said it was a bad copy of a bad copy of ancient Mongolian vertical script, probably a sort of shopping list, or perhaps a tally of people killed, towns pillaged, and atrocities committed.

She based this on the frequent reoccurrence of one symbol which she said was a corrupted version of the Mongolian symbol for death, and the fact that Ghenghiz Khan had skirted Brezakia in the 13th century.

But he was only one of many would-be conquerors of Brezakia. Alexander had paused at the base of the cliffs and decided it wasn't worth conquering. Attila the Hun had been in the region. After him, the Golden Horde and Tamerlane, the Persians and the Chinese, the Turks and Afghans had been there, but none of them had found a way onto the plateau. The Brezakian gene pool is neither Caucasian nor Asian, neither Turkic nor Arabic, Berber or Dravidian, but some other strain that broke off early in human history.

Dr. Stone's thesis was debunked by Professor Iosef Djindjinashvili of the University of Georgia in Tbilisi. "Djindjin" had been unable to decipher the manuscript and had passed it on to a logician acquaintance who sent it to Dr. Gustav Haammerstein (of the famous proof that all mathematical systems contain false, but unprovably false propositions which are undiscoverable, and at the same time true, but unprovably true, theorems (one of which, his detractors state, is his own proof, which rests on the argument that zero is not nothing, and neither is the blank symbol on a page, which he defines as the content of parentheses that have no content, namely ( ), but three nested parentheses is all a sane mind can take, so I end this digression here)).

Haamerstein, holding a cushy job in Einstein's old office at the Institute for Advanced Study at Princeton, fed it into a supercomputer, which concluded it was not a random number permutation, but a coded message corresponding to no known language or database. Not known to the supercomputer at least.

Haammerstein (privately called "Hammerhead" by his fellow advanced scholars) gave the photocopy to his eleven year old son on a rainy Sunday afternoon and told him it was the code to the location of Captain Kidd's treasure. Young Freidrich (awful name for a kid growing up in America, even in prim Princeton—we shall call him Fred) realized that if read diagonally, not vertically or horizontally, certain elements repeated themselves in a regular order and the treasure was buried in his own back yard.

After Haammerstein had disciplined Fred and ordered new sod, Fred realized it could be musical notation and decoded it this way, placing arbitrary notes for the symbols and submitted it to his sixth-grade music teacher as his own work (for which he was subsequently disciplined). The teacher, John Souser, arranged it for instruments playable by eleven-year olds (there are painfully few) and the resulting concert was described by one listener, an anonymous parent, as "reminiscent of a herd of berserk bull elephants on LSD stampeding through a boiler factory." Souser's contract was not renewed for the next school year, though it was not provably due to this incident, although the fact that the school board referred to it as an incident and not a concert was powerful evidence in itself.

But progress was being made. The musical transcript and Fred's key for deciphering it was mailed to a female friend of Souser's (they had gone to the same music school and once slept in the same bed, though at different times) with a letter lauding young Fred as the next Mozart. The colleague failed to notice it was postmarked April 1st. She passed it on to me, labeled "The Brezakian Symphony."

I have previously stated that it is impossible to go to Brezakia. But it is possible to come *from* there. I knew a man who grew up in Brezakia.

The man escaped in his late teens to see the world. At first he saw only Uzbekistan, a miserable part of the former Soviet Union, which, like most of its other miserable parts, had never wanted to be part of it. Later he saw China and India, where he learned passable English and procured a passable forged passport. In his thirties he came to the United States and worked as a translator for the U.N. since he was now fluent in seven languages. Then later worked, more sinistrally, for a security agency so clandestine its name is classified and its existence denied, to the extent that no one who knows of its existence is even allowed to deny it, as this would indicate there might be an agency whose existence was deniable, sort of a proof of existence itself.

It gave him ample funds and time, however, and with these he sought to recreate the instruments of his youth, the wooden cymbals, the brass drums, the bone piano, the stone xylophone, the ram's horn flute, the water hammer and so on (we will omit their Brezakian names, which would be unpronounceable consonants).

After twenty years he had assembled an orchestra of instruments in his basement. But no one but him knew how to play them.

He thought of using the agency's influence, which was not inconsiderable, to bring ten Brezakians to America. But they would not come willingly, the outer world being a great barbarism to Brezakians, and if kidnapped, they would not play their instruments well. A common Brezakianism is, "Breath comes from breathing," by which is meant, "One must do something willingly with one's whole being, without any external constraints or motivations, to do or have anything of lasting value and without lingering guilt feelings or the sense of having one's integrity compromised." Brezakian is a pithy language.

There was only one solution. He must teach foreigners to play Brezakian instruments. He began with his next door neighbor, a retired plumber. The old man had a facility with pipes, so he was trained on the bone flute, and could double on the water hammer.

By odd coincidence, his neighbor on the other side was a retired electrician. But he had really wanted to be a bassist. Wires are like strings. He took to the circular chicken gut rolling bass with a passion.

I passed the manuscript on to my Brezakian friend. He instantly recognized it as one of the great symphonies played for the summer solstice. The musical notation had symbols for each instrument and the note played, but the manuscript was not read horizontally, vertically or diagonally, but as a spiral out from the center.

I was invited to play one of the instruments, a kind of zither made from a sheep's thighbone and goat sinews, and after much practice our little band of mostly aged men was ready to play outdoors on Midsummer's eve.

In Brezakia, the entire population plays this symphony, from toddlers who can barely hold their instruments to oldsters who can barely hold theirs. The music goes on all night and through Midsummer's day and into the next night, accompanied by the universal drinking of their barley beer, brewed in barrels and kept only for this occasion and the Winter Solstice concert. Apart from these two events, Brezakians observe total abstinence. Anyone caught drinking at any other time is given the death penalty, defenestration off the cliffs surrounding the plateau, an elaborate ceremony accompanied by Brezakian music.

It is possible my friend fell into this category and managed to escape Brezakia's Death Row, though he never talked about it. He did, however, make a barrel of barley beer according to his secret Brezakian recipe, unbunged it on his back porch and insisted we drink generously of it as the music started.

This created some controversy as both his retired plumber and electrician neighbors were reformed alcoholics, but by telling them the beer was weak (a lie) he got them to imbibe. Other members of the orchestra, including myself, were robust and active alcoholics and tippled heartily.

The Brezakian tradition is to drink from a full ram's horn while also playing one's instrument and without spilling a drop. One cannot put the ram's horn down until it is empty.

I do not remember how our concert ended, or waking up in a jail cell as some of my less fortunate orchestra mates did. I do remember my Brezakian friend wildly gesticulating at me and saying, in broken Brezakian, in the mirror, that he made it all up and there was no Brezakia. I calmed him down sufficiently then wrote this down. Brezakia is real. Our music came from it. You hear it now. It echoes on strangely in our minds. It lingers past the ending of this story. It tells the story of a people isolated in central Asia, proud and tall, who believe in themselves and their heritage. They are a world inside our world. They have no crime, insanity or wars. Take a deep breath now. Let it out slowly. Breath comes from breathing.

Jocelyn Szczepaniak-Gillece

The Mandrake

"Mandrake, whose secrets grow seductively beneath the stone, I cannot uproot."

-Wolfgang Hilbig, "On Intonation"

We must have pulled it out too soon. It had grown in plain sight in the village square between the church and the ancient wooden stake whose purpose no one remembered. The top leaves seemed green enough to yank, but when we wrapped the dog's rope around it and beckoned the cur toward the fresh meat we held, the plant groaned, sent crumbled dirt and earthworms scattering, and let out a sound like the gates of hell cranking open.

The woman came tearing down the road, her hair like spiderwebs and her eyes blazing.

"Cover your ears!" she screamed. "It's not midnight and you have no ivory staff! You fools, cover your ears!"

The farmer's boy, the youngest of us, stared dumbfounded at her, his jaw slackening and his head tilting. At first he seemed frozen by fascination, but she was nothing more than a wise woman. Saliva poured from his open mouth and cascaded down his chin. His eyes rolled back in his head and he collapsed, shaking, on the ground.

"Stop them up! Stop up those holes in your heads, you idiots!" the woman shouted, throwing plugs of moss and clay at us, but it was so hard to hear her past the frantic high-pitched shriek rising up from the ground. Most of the plant's tangled roots were now up above the dirt, and they resembled a tiny hairy person with a wide-open mouth. Thick leaves sprang from the top of what looked like its head, a crowning glory above its desiccated skin.

The dog tipped over, dead before it hit the ground.

The youngest of us lay next to him, twitching slower and slower until his movements came to a complete stop and his head lolled unnaturally to the side, his tongue hanging out like a salted grey snail half-fled from its shell.

The plant's bellowing was a sonic death spiral, horrendous, wrapping us up in its whirlpool crescendo like an entire village burning to the ground. I couldn't think. I could barely see. I was turning to nothing but an enormous ear swiveling toward the uprooted plant and its stabbing exclamations. We were all becoming one in a wave of common pain.

I fell to my knees, my hands tearing out chunks of my hair, anything to feel something other than the sound like rivets pounding into my eardrums. It was an invasion, that noise, a cataclysm, Viking boats landing ashore and the pike and the torch with them. My brain no longer my brain.

Those of us farther from the plant and still with our wits about us grabbed at the moss where it hit us in the calves or the knees or the shoulders. Two plugs landed in a puddle by my right ankle and I grabbed at them and stuffed my headholes with them, sopping wet as they were, stinking as they were, those disgusting objects from a foul woman who smelled like powdered snake and dried rosemary and vinegar brine, nothing nice at all, nothing like the girls we wanted to marry and their lily-scented hair.

And instant relief washed over me. The kindness of silence, the bliss of the interior of my head being mine again. Dominion over my own territory.

The other young men of the village dotted the square, some still tearing maniacally at their bodies, some sitting down with plugs in their ears. The youngest and the dog lay dead next to one another. And between them, swallowing the light of the dawning sun like a black diamond, the wretched mandrake, tertiary roots like spindly ineffectual limbs, the hole in the middle of its face open in a bloated emission.

O f course I knew the danger. Mandrake hunting was not for the faint of heart. One must follow the old ways when harvesting the mandrake or risk the loss of his own life.

But I also knew that rarest of plants rewarded he who conquered it. The mandrake cured demonic ills, brought luck to its possessor, even bestowed the gift of the second sight for those brave enough to taste it. And those powers were of great value to magicians and traders alike. The mandrake was both curse and blessing, and most of all the mandrake was worth many times its weight in gold.

No one had pulled up a mandrake in years; from what I had been told, the mandrakes had all been harvested to extinction at least a century ago by sorcerers traveling west from the Urals, magi coming north from the lands below and across the sea.

If only they were found in our mountain village, then maybe we'd have fine plates and furs for trousseaus again. Maybe the children would come out strong from the womb, fed well on transmuted butterfat and thick cabbage leaves, rather than sickly and with yellow bags under their eyes. There might be hope, then, that the smartest among us would stay here after adolescence and help us all learn how to face the brave new world instead of hopping a carriage for Prague at the first opportunity and never returning home.

And then word came that a mandrake had been spotted on a hunting trip. Two young men from the village, alone with their bows for the first time, eyes glued to the ground for deer tracks, saw the telltale upright burst of leaves with emerald-tinged veins, the beginnings of exuberant purply flowers, a plant just begging to be tugged up from its rest.

They came back that day talking a mile a minute, about how they needed to read the manuscripts and gather up the boys. How this was the chance. Where there was one, there must be many. And where there were many, there was money.

"It would be better for everyone if they were all gone," the priest nodded when I asked him after matins. "Those who work in alchemy will never know God's presence. The light of Jesus makes a mockery of earthen magics and prestidigitation. See how I touch the host and it becomes his body."

The priest held the wafer up to the light, rosy and blue as it streamed through the stained glass window's filter. The wafer looked the same as it had a moment before. The priest covered it with a silken cloth and placed it in the tabernacle with a store of other consecrated breads ready for blessings or exorcisms.

"Don't go with them," he said. "It won't end well. You'll have to involve the woman."

The woman lived in the woods less than half a kilometer off the hunting trail. She had always been there, or a version of her had always been there; the cottage was a few hundred years old. Whether the woman was also a few hundred years old or she had merely taken the place of another woman in a succession of women was not for me to decide. It was enough to know that the woman held a place in a line that, despite its lack of maternal reproduction, was its own kind of genealogy.

Most of the time we pretended the woman wasn't there. You learned early on that when mention of her was made, you spat out of the left side of your mouth and rubbed the saliva into the dirt with your right foot. Every few months she came to the village market and sold her herbs and preserved vegetables for salt and blacksmith skills. She was tolerated then because there was a benefit to her appearance. Otherwise we ignored her as best we could except in very particular circumstances.

You went to the woman when you were in need.

Usually these were women's needs: fertility, romance, jealousy, desperation. Women have so many needs. A man rarely made his way there; if he did, he was sheepish and accompanied by a lover. But I wouldn't have been surprised to learn that most of the women in the village had, at some point or another, gone to see the woman. It wouldn't have surprised me at all.

My sister once had need of the woman and begged me to go with her. She was due to be married off in the fall to the widowed baker but through summer's long and lazy nights she had absconded many times with a boy from the village. Now there was a problem. If it wasn't solved, the priest wouldn't bless her marriage. Our mother couldn't know, she told me, our father would kill her. She couldn't go alone. She needed me.

My sister's voice was rich and pearlescent when she ululated in sonic shapes with other girls in the village. But she hadn't made much of any noise in days. She turned her dark eyes to me and they filled with tears. I couldn't bear my sister crying. I wanted to hear her sing again.

We pretended to join a small search party for a neighbor's goat gone missing and peeled off from the group to follow a dark path. The woods opened up and we stood in a little makeshift yard fenced in with squat posts and filled with wooden boxes of flowering salvias and monkshood, sprawling vegetable plants, and intricately carved birdhouses balanced on stakes. Goldfinches and nut hatches swooped through the elderberry and witch hazel and St. John's wort bushes came alive with hundreds of hungry bees. In the middle of all that abundance, the woman's thatched cottage stood with whitewashed walls and an array of painted flowers and calligraphy winding around every opening.

The woman came to the cottage door, her eyes on fire and her dress old-fashioned and her silver-streaked hair writhing all blue and electric like a nest of snakes. But her face was much younger than I thought it would be and she took my sister's small hand with her long and graceful one. I ducked behind a tree and waited for hours, tying blades of grass into wreathes and dozing under blossoming branches as the sun made its way through the sky. When my sister emerged, she looked exhausted but determined, and after we went home we never spoke of that afternoon again.

In short, I knew little of the woman, but what I did know was complicated by a dense thicket of secrets and love.

There seemed little left for us in the village. The priest collected our tithes and complained that we gave too little. Parents grew feeble and unable to work the fields. Children emerged with sores and cried through the night. The farmers fertilized the earth and spread last year's seeds in rows, but what came in summer was thin and diseased. We used it to feed our children and our parents and there was little left for us. We were all very tired.

I saw this future for myself and I didn't want it. I worked at my whittling and taught myself carving skills. I consolidated what I owned and consulted the carriage schedules for Prague. But then my sister married and soon had a new baby in her and I dreaded what would come next. Before I left the village, I determined, I would do what I could to make sure she sang again.

And so, although I had aided at the altar since I was a young boy, I didn't heed what the priest had to say. Not many of us really did beyond Sundays; we listened to his sermons, we gave him plum brandy when he came to our houses, we let him think he was essential. Though we didn't say it out loud, we knew that his approach was both useful and untrue.

When night turned to dawn, I packed up my carving knives and yesterday's loaf of bread from my sister's husband's oven and met the other men in the square. Together we turned toward the way I had walked the year before with my sister.

None of the men had been to the woman, at least none that wanted to own up to it. "This is the way, I think," the apprentice smith, the most confident of us, said, gesturing down the forest path. I kept quiet, because no one could ever make me betray my sister, and followed what I knew was the right way toward the woman's cottage.

All the birds fled in panic as the men sang drinking songs and hacked at underbrush. They tromped with heavy feet into the woman's garden and grabbed at the fruits ripening on the vine.

"Come out, woman!" the apprentice smith boomed, banging on the cottage door with the wooden end of a hatchet. "Tell us how to harvest the mandrake!"

Several other men threw coins the color of the woman's hair at the door as tradition demanded. The silver dropped to the stone step, clinking and sparkling in the sun.

A window's shutters flew open to reveal the top half of the woman. She stood there, bright against the interior gloom, stiff-shouldered like a statue, lips set in stone.

"I'll tell you," she said, "but I don't recommend this. You don't know how to do it nor even why you might."

"We'll sell it," the banker said. "Our money is old and worthless and we need new coins from new lands to buy the new things we need."

"We need new knives," the butcher said. "I've heard about some arriving from across the ocean, perfectly consistent from one to the next."

"We need new threshing machines," the farmer's boy said. "Those who use them have tender and soft hands and sleep past daybreak."

"We need new medicines," the apothecary attendant said. "Pills and capsules instead of dried herbs and tinctures."

"We need new fabrics," the tailor said. "Ones that shine and slip so that we no longer look like country people."

"We need a new altarpiece," the priest said, and all the men turned in shock to see that he had followed us on our journey.

"Yes, the church too has need," he said. "God is unchanged but the times are not."

The woman's lips stayed knit together and she paused for several moments. At last, she gave a curt nod.

"You'll regret it," she said. "But you'll forget it eventually. I'll regret this until I die. But I've already seen my fate and it is wrong to try to deceive destiny. Come with me."

The woman came outside with a leatherbound tome and a basket topped with moss. Together, we walked back along the pathway and into the forest.

"That's it, that's where it should be!" the apothecary attendant shouted, pointing at a withered stalk. The woman shook her head.

"What makes you think you know what mandrake looks like?" she sneered. "You fools. You have no idea."

The woman led the way and soon I realized we were walking back to the village.

The woman guided us to the town square and stopped across from the church steps and the stake.

"There," she said and pointed to her feet.

An unassuming cluster grew between two paving stones. If I'd noticed it, I'd have assumed it a weed. But now I could see the telltale fanlike shape, the fleshy and glossy leaves lined with celery-clear stems, the globular purple flowers almost obscene in their rich indigo, the yellow berries just starting to tempt birds.

"At the threshold of God's house," the priest murmured. "It must be a sign."

The apprentice smith ran over to the plant and bent down.

"No!" the woman shouted. "Not like that! You must follow the old ways. Yes," she said, staring at the priest, "even you."

And so the men noted what the woman told them was needed: a dog, a rope, fresh meat to tempt the dog, an ivory staff.

"Wait until midnight the next full moon," the woman instructed us. "It's a fortnight hence. But don't say I didn't warn you, and I won't say it when you come for me."

With that, she vanished back into the forest, leaving us clustered around the plant.

E ach of the men took turns standing guard for the next few days, making sure no drunk urinated on it, no goat came through and gnawed the leaves. It grew lusher and sent out more berries. The tailor shooed off the catbirds that tried to claim them. The priest blessed the site with the sign of the cross. Everyone searched their houses for an ivory staff.

But the men grew impatient. Farmers cursed their mildewed sprouts. Children cried for food that wasn't on the table. Wives begged for butter and thread. When a baby was born dead, its head barely attached to its spindly neck, impulse took over.

"Enough of this," the farmer's boy said. "My cousin will birth in two days and I can't have her baby come out like that, all green and still. It's time."

I said nothing, but I thought of my sister and the baby growing inside her. And so I gathered with the men in the small hours of the next morning as they dragged the mangy dog to the square and tied one end of a rope around it, the other end to the mandrake.

The sun began to rise.

The dog salivated and lunged toward the meat.

The mandrake sprang up from the ground.

And when the mandrake sprang up from the ground, it screamed like a banshee.

And when it screamed like a banshee, we were coursed with great pain and we too screamed with all our might.

And when we too screamed with all our might, a curious thing happened: my scream was my brother's scream was my brother's scream was my brother's scream.

And my brother's scream became mine in the common pain.

And the common pain radiated out from where the withered idol, the mandrake, lay among us.

And the mandrake lay among us until we came at last to our senses and gathered it up.

And we gathered it up with the youngest of us who lay there dead, and without ceremony we buried him.

And we buried him but left the dog to rot in the baking summer sun.

And in the baking summer sun all of us men felt a great and common rage rise within us, and the fury transformed us to a wretched black swarm, and we cursed the woman for her betrayal.

And her betrayal demanded punishment so we marched as one to her cottage.

And her cottage stood before us and we tore down the door, intent on dragging her out, but she had already donned her burial shroud and she held out her wrists to us so that we might bind her hands.

And her hands grew bloodied and raw with the pulling on the rope as we dragged her like a dog to the village square and the stake.

And the stake we knew now was always meant for the woman, and we tied her to her destiny atop a pile of wood, and the priest brought a candle from the church, and as we lit the woman on fire she cursed us all and her hair shone like dragonflies in the rising sparks.

And the rising sparks caught the church and the church blazed like the eyes of the woman.

And the woman and the church burned long through the night and in the morning.

And in the morning, we kicked at the ash left from the carcasses and uncovered the only smoldering remainder: the dog's jawbone.

And the dog's jawbone was taken up by all of us and lifted above our heads and nailed to the town gate.

And the town gate swung open and the road overflowed with horses and carts and people eager to buy and to sell and the world was full of things we were on the precipice of knowing and we bowed down in awe before the magnificent day that dawned upon us.

Laurie Blauner

Confessions of Furniture

The moon at the window stops to talk with my unmade bed. Both are empty or less than. *Leave me alone*, they both say at the same time.

You know what happened here, outside? I reply, pretending I am light and without artifice. I feign and feign as if my memory is an empty sleeve that needs filling. As if.

Sunlight dapples through pine trees outside, pouring through my window panes and onto a wall near a door downstairs. It resembles my child, changing, becoming different, but something. Before my husband left he offered me his chair, the one that carried our burdens, with its contrivances of sleep and resting. The seat took the shape of our missing child. My thoughts collect around that chair to remember who I had been. But, really, I want to forget and mostly I dream of snow blanketing everything, imitating the silhouette of whatever it covers. Grief is a thing, an object that I keep measuring as it varies.

Should I transform myself? I am staring at my green and white sofa which feels its own impermanence. The question implies fixing or repairing. A then, now, to be.

In Carrie's untouched room there are still the stuffed animals covering an upholstered chair, a miniature desk, thin colorful books, a pink pillow on a pink bed, a wooden dresser covered in stickers. They await a new life that I can't give them. The clock on the wall is still ticking. I don't want to give the furnishings any ideas while I can hear them breathing.

All else I converse with is quiet. But it feels as though the silence could explode and go in all different directions. My arms are vacant, unoccupied. In the living room cabinet there are keepsakes, a snow globe, a tiny bronze shoe, and a silver heart necklace. They don't know what to do. Maybe let go. In my mind my husband leaves again and again. Next time I want him to take everything.

I want to move soon. I am unsure what to do with all these possessions. I still love what I have lost. I lie down on her bed with the dead and it seems very ordinary. The moon keeps altering its outline as if it's wondering what's going to be left for it. I think about lifting furniture from its room into another house. To fill up someplace else. There, in the new place, maybe the dead will speak to me and explain everything.

ADDISON ZELLER

Land of Sunshine

Land of Sunshine. I don't remember which it is, Florida or California, but it sounds relaxing.

It's on a can of some goods or other, details forgotten, in a kitchen cabinet, visible only when my mother opens the door, in a house in my memory, thirty years ago.

I don't remember if it was the Spokane or the Gallup house. One received more sunshine than the other, being closer to the desert than to the ocean, but it also did not produce as a staple export any exotic fruit I know of.

A woman with a lowcut dress and frilly sleeves, a cap on her head, big earrings, and tiny feet is playing a long-necked instrument something between a mandolin and a theorbo on a toadstool as a jackrabbit leaps about dancing.

A dog walks up and sniffs the can sometimes when the kitchen cabinet door is open, right on the label. I laugh because a glinty imprint is left by the dog's nose on the woman's tiny fingers.

Over the rabbit's head, a flowering plant curls and resolves a bloom in a rising sun that casts rays into trees on either side of the composition. When I think of this can, I smell warm bark, specifically pinewood. I picture tiny floating pollen spores lit periodically by rays that pass between the tree branches.

I picture a hand opening and closing the cabinet door as more groceries pile onto the shelf that holds the can with the label I have remembered. A bag of rice thrusts not altogether patiently into a corner, disturbing a spider neither I nor my mother can see, but of which the dog, who can smell something unimaginable to us, the taurine scent of a spider, appears to my mind dimly aware.

I see the cabinet door open and close while objects pile on either side and sometimes, as with the bag of rice, lean against it. Whenever the cabinet door opens, I can smell the pine sap in my mind.

This was in either the Gallup or the Spokane house. If I were in either kitchen now, without knowing where I was, maybe I would recognize it, and maybe I would not.

If the can was still there, I would know what it was. If the rice was still there, I would know I was in the right kitchen. If the dog left its imprint on the label, I would know something inarticulable.

The preceding paragraph leaps from a straightforward statement of fact to a mystical sentimentalism unsupported by anything in the paragraphs that precede it.

If I recognized the instrument something between a mandolin and a theorbo at a concert or on the wall of a museum or in a music store it would confirm something inarticulable.

If I saw the dog again I would assume it was another dog. Even if the dog responded to the name that involuntarily escaped my lips, even if I knew in my heart it was the same dog, I would assume it was another dog.

If I saw and recognized the instrument something between a mandolin and a theorbo I would know something inarticulable.

Even to know this is to know that something.

NOAH DRAUSCHAK

Fable no.1—The Elephant's Burden

The Elephant stood shuddering as a mouse scurried between his feet. He dreaded not the mouse, nor fleas, nor possible pestilence. He dreaded that a single misstep could snuff an entire soul. Ashamed of his status & even more so of his trembling, the Elephant resolved to stand statue still till time could trample him instead.

Geoffrey Pitcher

Consumption

Why? I'll tell you why. Because I'm a testosteronite sextified by windows. That's why!

In my defense allow me to add that it was planned. The choreography was so subtle. I sit here knowing that I had been played. No!, not played, I had rather been engineered into a heightened state of testosteronexity. The architects knew exactly what they were doing. Looking back, they were ever so obvious in their subtlety. Because they knew, yes they knew. People want to go where they wanted to be led. You might say that my condition was therefore a product of my own volition. No No No!! Don't be fooled by the nostrum of willfulness. A ruse I tell you, a ruse!! My want was an inevitable consequence of larger manipulations. But before you file me into the swelling "victims" drawer to stew with the excess of whingers, note that I am not complaining. My tale is simply an exploration of the complexities involved when going just where you wanted to be led.

Cliché notwithstanding, it all started when I was but a child. Yes, the invisible hand puppeteered me right to where I wanted to be led from a tender age. And where was that you no doubt wonder with salacious curiosity? Beware, you literary pipmister, a detailed disclosure of my experience might just find you on lead as well! For all you know, I could be a puppeteer my own self, bedazzling you with your own unacknowledged wants to go just where you wanted to be led.

The windows were everywhere, some were wide open, some shut, some barricaded, others curtained. But it wasn't so much the extent of the exposure that they offered as it was the ubiquity of their presence. I do mean Everywhere! Incessantly dancing in my head with Seuss-like innocence and charm. Walking to school, playing pool, in the house, commanding my mouse, on my bed, in the shed, climbing the stairs, sitting on chairs, at the bar, driving the car, at the beach yet never within reach, on the table: "Eat me, I'm a bagel!" The exponential range and diversity of these want-scapes cannot be underestimated. For in the final analysis that is what they were: hollow apertures of desire, democratic vistas onto an ever-elusive nirvana.

Of course, this was all illusion, the imaginary rumblings of unsolicited desire. But the illusions magically transformed themselves from the imaginary to the real, cutting a pathway from the ethereal mind to the underbelly of my testeronicity gland, morphing from the illusional to make me delusional.

So what to do with all those unfulfilled projections into outer space? Thus the existential dilemma of the testosteronite brought to you by where you wanted to be led. Yeah, those head trips put a spell on me because they were mine. Brought to me by where I wanted to go no doubt, but mine and only mine. And should you doubt the extent and tenacity of their grip, I would ask you to consider routine spots of time in the testosteronic mind:

MOOD SWINGS

Ecstatic, the testosteronite sextified by windows celebrated his throbation.

Determined, the testosteronite sextified by windows indulged his throbation.

Confused, the testosteronite sextified by windows questioned his throbation.

Hungry, the testosteronite sextified by windows opened another tab.

Lonely, the testosteronite sextified by windows opened another tab.

Inquisitive, the testosteronite sextified by windows opened yet another tab.

Guilty, the testosteronite sextified by windows considered fapstinence.

Fapstinent, the testosteronite sextified by windows pined.

Pining, the testosteronite sextified by windows waxed glandular.

Glandular, the testosteronite sextified by windows clicked the mouse.

Accused, the testosteronite sextified by windows cleared his history.

Gloomy, the testosteronite sextified by windows cried "#MeTOO!!!"

Angry, the testosteronite sextified by windows cried "#MeTOO!!!"

Shocked, the testosteronite sextified by windows smashed the mirror.

Frightened, the testosteronite sextified by windows retracted.

Frozen, the testosteronite sextified by windows rebooted.

Don't laugh! Don't smirk! Don't degrade! Don't disdain! Most of all, DON'T JUDGE! I may be a testosteronite sextified by windows, but don't you be fooled: you're a player your own self. Ideologues of more hues than the rainbow cares to offer, health freaks, wellness gurus, gurvies and disciples: we're all taken in and betwizened by similar machinations, whether you care to know it or not.

So before you start your dirty digging, I would ask for a little empathy. These spots of time, windows their own selves, no doubt, reveal a disturbed sensibility. But the bottom line is that I was no Weinstein. In fact, I would argue that I'm an Everyman, or Woman, or They, if you must. This is not merely a manosphere predicament preying on hormonal vulgarians. My condition is that of everyone in the everyday be it at the gym, in school, at a PTA meeting or even in church. Imagine being in the grip of the fated mood swings while riveted to a pew. Let me tell you, testosteronexity takes the concept of Holy Raptures to a new level. But, and this is the point, and I don't have to tell you now do I: testosteronexity is a form of mental slavery. And as the man taught us all long ago, as such it exacts redemption.

But what then must be done? How to redeem yourself? How to fend off the subtle yet ceaseless manipulations brought to you by where you wanted to be led? A tall order when you consider what you are up against. We are, after all, talking here about the endless tease of algorithmic Hydras. Consumption in the Digital Age is a disease of a different color. This is not about I'll-do-you-one-better Conspicuous Consumption. Nor is it a direct consequence of mimetic desire. We've swerved deeply into the dependence effect, a world where desire has nothing to do with the simple satisfaction of individual need-wants and everything to do with the production of craving that at once feeds upon and nourishes its very existence. For the powers that take you where you wanted to be led incite you to relentlessly create your own desire. And just when you think you've done the very right thing, slammed the window shut and vanquished the lure of the want-scape, up pops yet another one. In the universe that brought you where you wanted to be led, the degenerate always and forever regenerates.

So I ask again: What then must be done? Do you devote yourself to eternal acts of extinction? Do you fast? Do you confess your want-vision sins and try to wipe the slate clean? Do you take refuge and seek rebirth in the Pure Land? Do you overcome through piety and prayers? How about a trip for the Cure? Will the Psychological White Plague tormenting you resist cod liver oil? Vinegar massages? Routine inhalations of hemlock and turpentine? Bleedings? Purging via emetics or enemas?

A smorgasbord of options.

I sampled each and every one of them.

They all left a foul aftertaste.

None of them worked!

And as I wallowed in my despair, what should happen? You guessed it, clever you! Up pops another window. As ever, my want conjured yet another scape. But this vista was different. Rather than luring me into the wanton testosteronic, it offered atonement, because this is where it knew that I wanted to be led. Dexterously circumventing testosteronic-fuelled desire, wellness windows started popping up everywhere. The promise of redemption lingered on the horizon: there was HOPE.

I started frantically clicking and exploring. And a whole new universe of self-help, care, and wellness began to unfold in a variety of forms and guises. Constellations offering improved health, emotional healing, fitness therapy, nutrition therapy, flotation therapy, mindful stress reduction, improved appearance, and even better sleep began to furnish my mental sphere. And while none of them addressed the specific symptoms of testosteronexity, they all led me to believe that help was on the way, if only I would commit to the expert counsel on offer.

So I tried, yes I tried. I clicked, I entered, I explored, I clicked some more, and some more, and then some more. And as I traveled into and through the labyrinth of possibilities, I began to feel overwhelmed. For rather than providing me with the wellness, relief, solace, and redemption that I so desired, the density of adjectives coaxing me toward a better self triggered my red-flag defense mechanism. The more I was confronted with rhetorical hooks saying "We take a head-on approach to psychological and physical wellness, guaranteeing results that will radically change the way you see the world and your approach to daily life," the more I began to doubt and distrust. Tell me, would you fall for the like of "Try the cryotherapy chamber for a major energy boost post-workout, or opt for something a little less bracing in the surprisingly calming hyperbaric oxygen chamber, which is said to improve cognitive function"? Hell no, you wouldn't! And I certainly didn't.

"Fuck this!" counseled my weary mouse. "Let me know if your Chakras ever agree to reveal themselves on an x-ray image."

I slumped back into my chair. And as I gestured my mouse toward unfulfilled closure, I noticed a faint spec of color dancing in the upper corner of my screen. Upon closer examination I discovered a butterfly. This was not just any butterfly, but one of the rarest of butterflies. It was a glasswing butterfly. And get this: it was lekking right at me! It had been quite some time since I had been lekked at, so I was understandably flattered. Flattered to the extent that despite my recent forays and ramblings, I clicked on the bait that its mere presence tendered.

Enter a world where the background hum of soft sotto "Om" has been replaced with the matter of fact resonance of "usque ad finem." A world of lush green leaves and plants. A world where butterflies fluttered, danced, and pirouetted with magnetic charm. A world where off in a corner basking in a wide ray of sunshine pouring down from a skylight, I saw an older, bald, Windsor-bespectacled man wearing a white lab coat. As he carefully placed long strips of bark in studied space, he became aware of my presence and looked up at me.

"Hello. And who might you be?"

"Hello," I replied. "I'm me, I guess. And who are you?"

"Oh excuse me for not introducing myself. My name is Stein. Some folks like to preface that with the honorific "Doc," but I don't go in much for formalities. I used to have a cabinet in Redemption Falls, but since the world seems to have moved ever the more out here into cyberspace, I closed up shop a few years back." Adding another piece of bark to the feeder, he continued. "As you have no doubt noticed, my obsession is with butterflies. I am simply and unapologetically infatuated with the variety of shapes, colors, and personalities that they exhibit. And what brings you to my corner of the infinite?"

"The simple answer is the lure of the glasswing butterfly that was strategically placed on my screen," I replied. "The more complicated response would relate to how the powers that know where I wanted to be led encouraged the glasswing butterfly to enter my sphere."

"Ahhhh those powers that know where you wanted to be led. I know a fair bit about them. In fact, you might say my professional life and reputation have been built on my various dealings with that crowd."

"Here I go again! No disrespect, Doc, but it seems to me that the powers that know where I wanted to be led have no doubt brought me to you. And I've had just about as much as I can take of going where I wanted to be led for one day."

Stein chuckled. "I know. I know. Those powers that led you where you wanted to go are relentless. But this said, in order to begin to understand your predicament, you need to recognize them for what they are: quite simply put, the powers that know where you want to be led are the unacknowledged legislators of the world."

"What?

Come again?

Say what, Doc?"

"Sounds a bit overwhelming, I know, but that's the bottom line. As you are beginning to realize, this is a force, a power, an emotional data bank, if you will, that we internalize by and for ourselves. And it can and often does take on a Frankensteinian life of its own that wreaks havoc on people like yourself. Don't ever forget that

the architecture of thoughts comes in fragments of vision
scaffolds of "empirical" wisdom
conjured by desire

the building thus
raised with suspect mortar

for desire is a fickle friend at best
leaving us always and forever
WANTING

So, and as I always ask each and every pilgrim
who ends up here seeking redemption: How
does it feel to want?"

"How does it feel to want? Very funny, Doc!
The answer to your rhetorical question lies in the
derisive grin on your face: It sucks! But before
you lead me to the couch to explore and evaluate
the fabric of my personal experience with desire
while simultaneously weeding the green leaves
from my wallet, let's cut to the chase. You know
what I want now? I want OUT! So please, Doc,
beam me outta here!" My eyes gestured upward,
frantically searching for an escape hatch.

"You want out? Beam you out of here? Bad
news, Pilgrim: there's no exit from the gift shop.
You're in it for the long haul. There isn't a rem-
edy. You can't be cured from going where you
wanted to be led. What you do need at this very
moment is to cross the shadow line and realize
that the question is not how to escape your condition but rather how to live with it! Trust me Pilgrim: therein lies the path to your redemption."

"No exit? What? This is the forever forever?
No wellness to ever be seen or had? No solace?
No redemption? A testostronite for life?

"Don't wax so forlorn, Pilgrim. This doesn't
have to be viewed as a one-way ticket to hell with
an overnight stop in purgatory. For all you know
I could be the bearer of liberating news. Crossing that shadow line forces you to adjust your
spectacles, see things in a different light, consider other possibilities. That sort of thing. You
exhibit a condition that is shared by all who venture into my lair. You see want as a debilitating
disease. "It sucks!" I believe you said, with the
implication that it is destroying you. What I

would simply ask is that you reconsider this
ever-so-human emotion. It doesn't have to be a
destructive force. It could, in fact, be the opposite. Think about it: Wanting can actually feel
pretty good. It gives you energy. It's motivating.
It makes you feel alive. Surely you would agree
that it is better than having and not wanting, the
very stuff of ennui, torpidity, stupor, mental
laziness. No, no, no, Pilgrim, sad satiety must be
avoided at all costs. You need to immerse yourself in the constructive element."

After a long and thoughtful pause, I lifted my
head and looked Stein in the eye: "Let me get this
straight, Doc: Are you telling me that my redemption is to be found in the very incessant
clicking that's been consuming me?"

"Not quite, Pilgrim: I'm suggesting that the
incessant clicking that's been consuming you is
rooted in a vacuum, an emptiness that you try to
fill with new possibilities. And in this world
there is no short supply of what we assume are
new possibilities. You're in a rut that you think is
a byproduct of testosteronexity, but in fact
testosteronexity is a symptom of a larger illness.
Consumption festers in people lacking sustained, passionate focus. Your problem, dear
Pilgrim, is not that you want incessantly, but
rather that you don't know what you want!!

"Believe me, I know what I'm talking about. I
was likewise my own self, until my butterfly
mind settled on, well, as you can see, on BUT-
TERFLIES!"

CODA

Of course the best time to gather them is in July
and August after a heavy rainfall. They'll have
been fattened up by the spring shoots and
growth by then. Lidded container in hand, I like
to go searching for them in the early morning or
during a digestive after-dinner stroll. Avoid the
likes of roadsides and train tracks where pesti-
cides may have been sprayed. Make sure that you
gather the ones with the thick hardened ridges.
They'll be fully mature and best for stewing.
Some people say you need to starve them for a
couple of weeks, but I'm not into such torture.
Rather, I regularly feed them organic, whole
wheat flower for intestinal detox.

After they've been purged, soak them in some warm water mixed with a fair bit of red wine vinegar. Then drain them in a cauldron and thoroughly rinse them under cold water. Get the goodies that will be joining them ready: chopped shallots, diced garlic (be more liberal than you can imagine with the number of cloves), 300-600 (depending on the size of the catch) grams of sausage meat (if you can't find this, substitute it with thick bacon). Chop up a bouquet of parsley, and join that with freshly cut thyme and rosemary and some bay leaf. In a large heated sauce pot, either drop a healthy dollop of butter or pour a charitable dose of olive oil. Brown the shallots and then put in the sausage meat. After braising the meat, douse it with Cognac, and burn baby burn. When the flame has dissipated, tip the

cauldron into the pot
tents. Cover this with
that is rich in Syrah
but to each his own).
herbs and bring to a
heat to a low simmer,
patiently,   pa-
ingredients blend into
harmonious   melting
taste and serve in soup
brown bread on the
choice.

and empty the con-
red wine (I like a wine
and Grenache grapes,
Put in the garlic and
boil. Turn down the
and   patiently,
tiently   let the various
an active and ever so
pot. Salt and pepper to
bowls with thick heavy
side   and   tipple   of

Bon appétit

©J.VILLEGIER

Stéphane Marteau, Héliculture. Jacques Villegier, 2010

DJ Huppatz

Satoshi

I'd just finished the first verse of *Born in the USA* in Chengdu's biggest karaoke complex when my phone buzzed. I handed the mic to Chen.

They were moving the mine. I had to take the call.

"Where, Jerry, where?" I yelled as I closed the door behind me.

"Kazakhstan," Jerry replied.

At that single word, my dreams of sitting down to a plate of ribs at Big Daddy Ray's Smokehouse or sipping a margarita under a palm tree by the beach after work vanished. I slumped onto the corridor's mirrored wall.

"What?"

"I know, Noah, I know. Believe me, I was rooting for Texas too. And, FYI, El Salvador was never a viable option. Sure, it's disappointing but think of this as an opportunity. Kazakhstan's just across the border. Not too hot, not too cold. Cheap electricity."

"So, you've organized the trucks?"

"Trucks could get held up at the border. The hash rate's already dropped twenty percent. We don't want to be frozen in deeper. We've chartered a plane for you. Be ready by Friday."

"Friday? What do I tell the crew?"

"Remind them of the relocation bonus. Remind them that they used to move the mine up to Inner Mongolia every Fall. Trust me, it'll be fine. Dmitry, our man on the ground, will help with anything you need when you get to Kazakhstan."

I put the phone back in my pocket and my mind whirled. The corridor's mirrored walls sparkled with colored light. It was like standing in a kaleidoscope.

Less than a week. Fifteen thousand machines. I glimpsed a fragment of my face on the opposite wall and watched bits of me bouncing back and forth down the corridor.

It could wait until morning.

I opened the door as Chen was fist-pumping through Springsteen's last chorus as the guys cheered and held up beers. I typed the words *I Will Survive* into the karaoke machine.

On Friday afternoon, we landed at an abandoned military airbase in an empty valley where a local team loaded our machines into waiting trucks. They drove us over the valley's edge and into another, then along a winding dirt road to the Anthill: eight shiny sheds on a dusty plain. Behind them sat a dorm, a canteen, and a transformer station. A line of skeletal transmission towers snaked into the distant mountains.

The Kazakh team, who spoke neither English nor Chinese, unpacked the Bitminers and stacked them into the floor-to-ceiling racks that lined each shed, working in shifts day and night. We had the mine operational in less than three days and settled into our regular routines.

We ran the machines at full capacity, twenty-four hours a day, every day. Repairing, cleaning, cooling, monitoring. Meanwhile, coders in Austin and Seattle nudged and tweaked their algorithm envelopes in infinitesimal steps, hoping for that one in 16 trillion sequence that delivers the final block.

A week after our arrival, I was drinking my morning coffee outside the dorm when I noticed a dust cloud on the horizon. It gradually morphed into three men on horseback. They slowed as they approached. The lead rider, on a large, chestnut horse with a blonde mane, dismounted in front of me. He wore a black t-shirt and combat pants. Wraparound, mirrored sunglasses sat on his flinty cheekbones.

"Welcome to the Free World! I am Dmitry Ivanov," he said as he shook my hand firmly.

"Do you have everything you need? What else? A football pitch? Basketball court? Vodka? Women? Anything. Just let me know."

The other two riders dismounted and stood behind Dmitry. They wore matching blue Adidas tracksuits. Tattoos crept up their necks. Each had an assault rifle strapped over a shoulder.

"Everything's fine," I replied. "But there's one thing the guys miss."

"What's that?"

"Karaoke. A Karaoke machine would be great."

Dmitry laughed, turned to the two men behind him, and translated. My request raised a smile.

"Yes," he said, "I can arrange that."

He remounted and the trio rode off in the direction they'd come from.

F ive years ago, Jerry entrusted me with my first mine.

"That'll be you soon," he said, pointing to a framed photograph on his office wall. It was the famous shot he commissioned after he'd made his first million. Grinning under a black floppy hat, he wore a checked shirt and held a pickaxe over his shoulder.

"You're coming to China too, right?" I asked.

Jerry poured two whiskeys from a crystal bottle.

"Noah, Noah. You know the machines. You speak Chinese. It'll be just for a year or so. Just until we get established. Believe me, this is an opportunity."

I believed him. In a year or so, I thought, I'll be back here driving a 911, dating influencers, and drinking cocktails by my pool.

He raised his glass.

"To Satoshi!"

"Who?" I asked.

"Satoshi Nakamoto. Our inspiration. Our patron saint. Some say he's a reclusive Japanese coder who died years ago. Others say he's a physicist living off the grid in Oregon. Some even believe it's the code name of a top-secret government cryptography team. All we know for sure is his last message was delivered in 2011."

Jerry read from a framed quote on the wall.

"*The root problem with conventional currency is all the trust that's required to make it work.* Note the keyword, Noah: *trust*. That's why I need you in China."

Years later, in the Chengdu karaoke complex, I told Chen about the mysterious Satoshi.

He laughed.

"Satoshi is the name of the great Pokémon trainer."

"Satoshi?"

"English name Ash Ketchum."

"And what about Nakamoto?"

"A Japanese philosopher. Famous for *mukishinron*: no gods or demons."

"So the name's a joke? He doesn't exist?"

"I'm not saying that Satoshi Nakamoto doesn't exist."

"How do you know all this?"

Chen smiled in his enigmatic way, took the mic from me, and began to sing.

T he day after we met Dmitry, a Kazakh team arrived. They assembled a large, round wooden frame, covered it in white animal hide, then painted the hide with red waves. As the outside dried, they carpeted the interior, strung fairy lights from the supports, and hung a central mirror ball. Finally, they installed a state-of-the-art karaoke machine.

This was our Karaoke Yurt.

On any night of the week, Chen would crouch over the mic, stomping his feet in time, thrusting his hips back and forth as the repair guys joined in the chorus:

"I LOVE TAIWANESE GIRLS."

Next Hou, the cleaner, would get on the mic, make a "raise the roof" gesture, and launch into "Fly to Other People's Beds". Then Han would launch into his hip-hop cover of "The East is Red", marching and saluting in time before Yu calmed us down with a ballad.

"Two heroic flowers," sang Yu, gripping the mic with two hands, "sacrificed their lives. No chance to blossom. Tears drop from every eye."

Occasionally they did.

One night, in the middle of *Born to Run*, my phone buzzed. It was Jerry. I handed the mic to Chen.

"Jerry! What's up?"

"The board's spooked. The hash rate's tumbling, the reward's halved."

"Jerry, what are you saying?"

"Going forward, the Anthill is not part of the ongoing mix."

"Wait, what?"

"They sold it."

"Sold it? Who to?"

"The Russians. Dmitry's the new owner."

"Don't tell me, this is an opportunity, right?"

"Noah. Trust me, you'll be fine."

A few days later, just before dawn, a convoy of trucks arrived and a Kazakh team laid foundations for four new sheds. They returned the next day, competed the sheds and filled them with banks of Russian-made machines. When they were done, Dmitry and his two guys rode in on horseback. As before, he dismounted in front of me with a hearty handshake.

"How do you like your new machines?"

"Nice," I replied, "but we're already at capacity."

He smiled. "Our coders in Petersburg work twenty-four and seven."

"Yes, but the problem is . . ." I started.

"There is no problem. Here's your new roster," he said, handing me a piece of paper.

"But the guys are working around the clock already."

"Let them sing," he replied. He repeated the line in Russian for the amusement of his men.

Then he mounted his great chestnut horse, and the trio rode away.

Fifty percent more machines meant fifty percent more errors, fifty percent more repairs, fifty percent more cables, and fifty percent more fans to dust. I examined Dmitry's new roster. The shifts were longer, and he'd cut our nightly karaoke sessions to just one on a Saturday night.

I heard only shouting as I approached the Yurt. "There's too much dust getting in the machines. You're too slow!"

"Too slow? We've an extra four sheds to clean."

"Remember the old saying, 'the clumsy one needs to start early!'"

Yu, the gentle ballad singer, leapt at Han and wrestled him to the ground.

Chen and I pulled them apart.

"Let's get out of this damned country," yelled someone.

"We're in the middle of a desert," someone replied.

"I say we wait for the next delivery, jump the Kazakhs, and drive their truck home."

"I say we stop work until we get more crew."

"Don't be stupid. I need to send money home. My family's counting on me."

"Fine then. Stay and live like a dog in the desert!"

I was relieved when Chen tapped the mic and the crew stopped arguing to listen.

"The dragon at low tide waits for the water to rise," he said. "Until then, let's sing."

He dialled up *Hey Jude*. It was an inspired choice. By the end, everyone was singing.

The next morning, the crew worked in silence. Strangely, Chen seemed cheery, whistling *Hey Jude* as he worked. I asked him if he was OK.

"He's coming," replied Chen.

"Who's coming?"

He just smiled his enigmatic smile.

I was drinking my morning coffee outside the dorm when a dust cloud appeared on the horizon. Two riders approached. Dmitry's thugs dismounted, tied up their horses, and sat on folding chairs outside the dorm. They spent the morning drinking vodka, occasionally poking their rifles into the sheds and yelling in Russian. They dozed in their chairs all afternoon then, just before dusk, rose and rode off towards the distant mountains.

Every day they came. Every day the same.

The Russian-made machines, fast at first, broke down often. We couldn't keep up.

For some reason, I remember it was a Friday morning when Hou, the cleaner, put down his mop and refused to work anymore. Dmitry's thugs shouted at him in Russian and prodded him with their rifles. Hou just sat there cross-legged on the shed floor. Then Han joined him. Soon, six of the crew sat on the floor and more came from the other sheds.

Dmitry's thugs went outside. I watched as one of them took a full vodka bottle and doused our Karaoke yurt. The other lit a match and flicked it onto the wet hide. Blue flames leapt up the yurt. The crew gathered to watch it burn but Chen ushered them into the dorm. I told everyone to take the afternoon off and rest. I'd think of something. Strangely, Chen didn't seem worried.

I sat outside drinking coffee.

Dmitry's thugs were hunting for food in the canteen. I faced my chair away from the black hole where the yurt used to be and studied the crinkled mountaintops in the distance. Then a dust cloud appeared. A single rider. As he got closer, I could see the distinctive chestnut horse with a blonde mane. But the rider wasn't Dmitry.

It was a tall, thin man with dark, spiked hair, in a long, black coat. His eyes were like inky coals set deep in his head. As he dismounted in front of me, I glimpsed the pearly grips of his revolvers holstered on each hip.

"I am Satoshi Nakamoto," he said, as he shook my hand.

"But I . . ." I began.

He raised his hand and shook his head.

Dmitry's men emerged from the canteen, fumbling their rifles. Satoshi cooly drew both guns from his holsters and took aim. A stream of fire leapt from each gun with a crack. The two thugs slumped backwards into the dust.

Satoshi blew the blue smoke from the end of each barrel and re-holstered his revolvers.

A convoy of trucks rolled into the Anthill, and he signalled to us to get in.

"But the mine . . ." I started.

Satoshi shook his head.

As Chen herded the crew into the trucks, Satoshi Nakamoto mounted the great chestnut horse with the blonde mane and waved us off. Once the trucks had crossed the plain and risen onto the first hill, we heard an explosion. We turned back to watch the Anthill erupt into a smoke cloud that puffed out across the sky before raining down millions of bits across the Kazakh desert.

Fiona O'Connor

There's Always Something

The big studio in cold light. Empty space to be zig-zagged by the regiment. In fear, always.

Naked, only a lycra veneer like you were a basted chicken.

Brightness in off the Hudson. The studio mirror a silver tributary spanning lengthways. Space sullen in its detachment, in its thingness, haecceity or something.

Gesture swimming up to the harmonies, swirling in time: rhythm intensifiers, curt to the beat. Only allure dowsed the rigidity of a ¾ time signature through their spines.

There was no we: single combat; only you and the soldier in the mirror.

So she thinks anyway, on the A line downtown, looking sideways, nodding her head to agree, seeing and not seeing a pair of chestnut riding boots and the man in them asks a question that she makes some attempt to answer before it even registers, and his eyes and her eyes see themselves.

So he gets off the subway at her stop, Gramercy, and she lets him walk beside her, along the platform, up the steps, on up the steps again to the street. He's talking with an English accent not heard in a long time: northern vowels in a deep bass-baritone voice.

The street is swarming with workers getting home. Still it is so. It is forever so.

What's his name? Give him a name.

Duncan.

He will take her to dinner—'tack'er' is how he pronounces it. 'Dinnah'.

Pick'er up?

No. She will meet him there. So she has a get out and will probably use it.

But she doesn't. She finds herself before another mirror stroking mascara along her lashes.

There's a cat, not hers; she's to feed it before she leaves. Does the cat have a name? Archie can be the cat's name. She glares at the cat tray, not yet soiled.

These things trail out, arrive a disappointment.

She will arrive a disappointment. At the restaurant, late but not enough.

Maybe he'd inflated the ideal. The long-haired thin girl with straight back and sharp calves.

Sees the start of a bitter pinch to her facial expression. Sees the beginnings of a downturn at the mouth, and her face grey-tinged perhaps.

He wears a brown suede jacket and has changed into a brown shirt. With fat fingers he sweeps his thinning brown hair to the side. He is a little nervous because of his wife who he telephoned from the hotel before leaving. So she wouldn't go calling for him later.

Because he might be busy. He thinks not, in all probability. This is not his usual sort of adventure; hasn't done it before actually. Although he has never before been so far away from his wife.

I didn't think you'd come.

They drink wine. They eat steak.

I nearly didn't.

He plays down his stint in Afghanistan although he had killed a man there.

And then I went into the Horse Guards.

She nods her head looking at the tablecloth.

A soldier was left behind in the mirror too. A spike driven into the floor, ramrod. Toes are crushed, insteps catching the gun-barrel light. On up to the arms outstretched as though in appeal to the one who looked. And turn. In an instant turn. And run. And *bourrée* rapid fire, till another takes her place.

But to Duncan, she was a mouse of sloping shoulders, challenged by her steak, sawing and pulling for minutes until he had to put down his own knife and fork.

Here, can I?

It's a bit . . .

I know. But try some of these smaller bits.

Yes, ok.

And the obedience in her face as she chewed and chewed.

Because he knew nothing of her perfect *en pointe* triple turns. Manifested: risen perfection when the notes crowned.

He knew, could know, nothing of this.

Which was part of the lone-ness she occupied, as any soldier knows.

He said he'd tak'er back to Gramercy—*Graam-acy*; he was going that way, to us 'otel, like.

The sales team boys he was with would spot them if he brought her there. He didn't say it but she knew, of course she knew. She'd been in the city over two years: she got things quick. Especially of desire. Especially of aspiration—the city screamed it out day and night.

She went to the restrooms leaving him to get the check. In the closet she brought up the meal without making a sound. She flushed, waited, flushed again, rinsed her mouth out before another mirror—the mirror of her inmate self: the lurker, so called.

She watched as she dried her hands in her hair, running wet fingers from the roots, pulling her face tight, her eyes aslant—how she would like to look if she was right.

Grasping her hair like rope, twisting it into a high ponytail held in her left hand, a rise into *relevé* then, pulling herself up by the tail, posed like a flint, and holding the pose staring into herself. Who stared at who—soldier or lurker, lurker or soldier, impossible to decide.

He, Duncan, went nestling too close in the taxi. Cab ride of a loving couple bumping up 8th. Not two strangers pulled from the A train earlier, magnetised into each other's orbit out of the stir, the menage ranging, dodging and desperate, through the island.

She pointed to something on the street. He pretended to be amused. She was aware of a sumptuous warmth she could sink into: dense substance of body adjoining hers.

But a soldier is never off duty.

Yet the closeness to flesh that was not striving to kill itself, was only meat which had arrived to full density, without thought, or fear, without concern: this was novel. And so missed without realising that she felt a sob rising in her throat.

She saw their yellow cab wipe across black glass but failed to catch herself looking.

For the viewer a *pirouette* sprang up like a steely plume but in its making was a heaviness you had to camouflage. Preparation was down into the earth, the body locking onto its forces, the burden you mustn't show. Would it work, your turn? You never knew, only trust in the preparation. Split second before springing up through the spine and backwards into the clockwise revolve like into a fall, returning to front, again, again, again, till rhythm unwound and you came down, smile burnishing a glister in the spotlights.

Not thinking of what you'd eat and puke.

He was there in her space, the cat rubbing itself against his legs. She smelt the shit in the cat litter, thought the automatic not fair of the tray always stinking up her section—tiny kitchenette with the jammed in sofa as her bed.

I'll get rid of this.

He, Duncan, took off his suede jacket, laid it over the sofa arm, sat back on the sofa, pushed the cat away.

She took the cat tray into the bathroom. Saw herself in the bathroom, flushed the cat shit, left the tray in the shower stall.

Looked at herself again. Where was soldier? Where was anybody?

She'd a whole weekend to survive. Survival was starvation. She'd only herself to deny.

Nice boots.

He'd crossed his right leg over the left when she came out of the bathroom so it was something to say.

'andmade. He stretched out the leg as though to check. Chelsea boots, he said. He sold saddlery. That was his job.

The thought of it was depressing. A job. When she was a soldier. Not a job: an *a priori*. Her sexuality she'd refined to a quiver, to an impossibility, to a take-no-prisoners full scale campaign against every dissenting impetus the lurker could muster.

Nice, she repeated.

Come 'ere, he beckoned her.

She was standing in front of him. He thought a bit dejected-looking.

Sitting then standing. Drink? she asked.

There was some beer in the fridge belonging to her roommate. She darted to the fridge before he answered.

We can share, he said, taking the bottle from her. She noticed his Adams apple moving when he swallowed. The skin of his throat in the opening of the brown shirt collar was wrinkled. She smirked.

What?

Nothing. Just the cat. He likes you.

Cats always like me because I don't like them.

I don't like them either.

So why?

Not mine. It's my roommate's. Her apartment.

Ah. Where is she?

Away. At her boyfriend's place. She won't be back.

Good.

Why do you say that?

They smirked. Sitting on the sofa looking towards the kitchenette.

Because I want to get to know you.

Like a horse?

At the restaurant he'd told her about his horses, how he trained them, got their trust, even the difficult ones, how they followed him around the yard after a while.

No, not like that.

She twiddled the beer cap feeling its crenulated edges against her fingertips. She pressed the hard edges into her palm, then onto her inner wrist, making marks on her skin. Glancing down—it looked like a tutu skirt. She pressed harder, secretly, over her pulse spot. It was a good feeling, cutting the blue-veined throb with gold-coloured metal. It was where she was, her edge.

Reciprocating pain was where you found yourself, as a soldier.

How did these games get in, she thought. Her own performance offended her. But she wouldn't change it. You don't; you can't change the choreography you've been given. Discipline. At least that, she thought.

She watched his throat swallowing again. The yellow beer in the bottle in his hand held against the brown mound of his gut. He rumbled on. His words were brown too, she realised.

He was telling her he'd be back soon. He'd be coming over every few weeks because now they had this new contract.

She didn't say it but she had no contract—it was her greatest lack. She was hanging on the periphery of the ballet company in hope of a contract, and had been working in a restaurant dodging between the fat chef and the fat owner getting her orders: club sandwiches, burgers, steak-fries, squeezing herself like paper between two disgusting men, and she had recently been fired for pocketing cash when one of them saw and told the other, and now her roommate was hinting that she should move out, no, not hinting—telling.

She didn't have a contract—it was a catastrophe. So she didn't care if he came back or not.

Come 'ere. He pulled her into his torso, held her there. Breathing in and out, swelling and collapsing, swelling and collapsing, like the velour sofa was a tide.

Yer alright pet.

Look at me.

Look at me.

Yer alright. Ok?

She took him into the roommate's room, into her bed.

And it was like mounting a shire horse—his hips so wide. She rode the wide hips, the wide torso underneath her. She smeared herself over his chest. She found the small penis put into her; let it be.

Talking through the whole ride. To herself. Because he had to listen so she talked.

Yesterday I gained I know I did but I reduced today I was still down this after . . . but it might go back on I don't know I'll see I'll have to see if it does—if it's back in the morning what? I'll have to see it depends I don't know I might not have it might not—check in the morning before everything this is the worst time but I don't feel it so bad because I brought it all up I brought up everything I think so but you know there's always something there's always something . . .

He moaned. She glanced down at him. She moved on his moans, trained soldier as she was.

He tried to stop himself, his panting sounds low hoofbeats cantering away from him—he had never . . . he had never . . .

She rode the rhythm, expert to the beat, to the throb of a heart somewhere.

GREGORY FEELEY

PETRAGLYPHE

Homage à R. A. Lafferty

Socrates says in *Meno* that the statues created by Daedalus were so skillfully made that they would run away if not tied down. But how would he know that, unless it had actually happened?

And were those that escaped caught and brought back? Of course not, for a statue that leaps off its pedestal and sprints for the door has a several seconds' drop on its startled creator, mallet still in hand. This is not to mention their incentive to flee, for a sculptor's studio offers ample evidence of what becomes of a statue who lets pass the opportunity offered in that instant of creation, when *kaos* has not yet shivered into *kosmos*.

Cleitus was the first, though that was only the name he gave himself later when he needed one. He had had the wit to run downhill, which lent speed to his flight. This took him to Herakleion and the docks, where he disappeared into the crowd—a naked man being less conspicuous among laborers than in the artisans' quarter—and quickly sought work as a deckhand on a trading vessel preparing to load.

The captain he approached was struck by his appearance, for Daedalus had created the likeness of a god, or at least a hero. He asked the statue's name and the fugitive, breast swelling but hardly out of breath (for how can a statue be winded?), spoke its first word. "Kleitos," he said, a name it had heard one of its pursuers shout to another.

"Cleitus, I like the cut of your jib," the captain replied. "Your features seem a bit disfigured—" for the sculptor had not yet effaced the cuts of the chisel—"but you look right fit for hauling sacks and pulling lines. Come aboard."

When he saw how the gangplank bent beneath the statue's weight, he was only momentarily discomfited. "Better yet—ballast that can load itself! You can lie down snug in the hold, and I bet you don't eat much, either."

So Cleitus took berth on a ploion bound for the Cyclades with a cargo of grain and wine. Two days out they encountered a storm and the ship went down with all hands. Some sailors clung to the wreckage, hoping perhaps for a dolphin to deliver them to shore, but Cleitus sank straight to the bottom.

He landed up to his knees in crusty sediment and stood staring in the virtual darkness. The ship, trailing bubbles like a comet, came to rest nearly atop him, and when the cloud of silt settled he felt along its length and guessed that its prow lay in the direction they had been headed. He set out forthwith, and may someday emerge on a beach on Naxos, richly garbed in barnacles and perhaps bearing treasure from the shipwrecks he has passed.

But it was the second statue that fled inland, into the hills. Athena knew well what her name was, for she had heard it murmured reverently as the lineaments of her bare arms were pumiced smooth. She had even greater impetus to speed her, for men snatched at the hem of her flying chiton, and Daedalus, who could be *ekpiktos* once but not twice, had left unpainted one of her eyes when he loosened the leather thongs that bound her feet in order to finish her toes. Half sightless and still trailing a cord twining her ankles, she tore free the garment from the first man who seized it, but when two caught hold in a lucky grab, she had no recourse but to twist and slip free of it, leaving behind their outraged shouts as she raced uphill, dressed only in her kestos.

There were no city walls in the days of King Minos, for who would dare attack an island that was guarded by Talos? Perhaps the brass automaton declined to remark unfamiliar figures seeking to *depart* the city, or else perhaps it felt a curious kinship with a creature wrought by craft from lifeless matter. She veered from road to path, crossed orchards and fields, and vanished into the foothills south of Knossos.

The mountains of an Aegean isle are no safe place for any young woman, let alone one dressed as she was. Athena sought to readjust her garment so that it covered her loins rather than her breasts, but her appearance remained an incitement to any creature that could outrun her, a group that excluded men but admitted much else.

Indeed, she was not half an hour in the forest when the high-scudding clouds parted to release a shaft of sunlight, and a flash of marble-white caught the eye of a *satyros*. No scent touched its twitching nostrils, but the thicket-shaded eyes of the creature, who was named Porkos—his mother knew him for what he was—widened in recognition. In an instant he had burst from the underbrush and, heedless of the noise he made (satyrs do not rely upon stealth), was pelting across the meadow toward his intended victim. That such a deformed creature could run so fast! As though his race had been created as a warning to nymphs to keep close to the safety of their tutelary tree or stream.

Athena was able to reach the edge of the trees before he brought her down, and he dragged her without ceremony into a clearing. What followed was variously retold for centuries. Sappho wrote of it, and so (rather differently) did Aristophanes. Neither account has survived the ravages of time, but the Aegean world's remaining nymphs, those pegaeae and limnades whose lakes and streams still endure, recount what happens when you seek to violate a stone maiden. Listen carefully and you can hear their burbling laughter.

For Porkos, of course, it was no laughing matter. "What manner of monster are you?" he cried in pain and fury as he rolled about miserably.

"I am Athena," she said simply, backing away to a safe distance.

"You are an affront to my very nature," he retorted. And because satyrs can think well enough when their throbbing kaprophalloi are momentarily disabled, Porkos added, "In truth you are a *pseudos*, a semblance of comeliness."

"The comeliness seems real," she replied.

"And your name stinks of hubris. Give yourself another one, lithokolpos, ere the true Athena learns of your presumption and punishes you more grievously than you have me."

"I have no other name," the statue replied. But in renouncing her own, she lay open to being named by another, and she did not wish to be known for having a stone *kolpos*. Quickly she added, "I am Petraglyphe, the maiden of stone, and I take up this branch to thrash you—" which she proceeded to do before the wretched beast could scramble to his feet—"until you persuade the nymphs of these fields to come forth and aid me in my distress."

And Porkos was compelled to beseech the nymphs he had long molested to render succor to their fellow woman. He had nothing to offer them save his promise to assail them no more, which they enforced by binding him with vines to a tree. (They vowed to keep him thus, replacing the vines regularly, for the next several decades.) Then they wove for Petraglyphe a peplos made of leaves and a himation made of coarse grasses. They daubed her unpainted eye with pomegranate juice mixed with the sap of opuntia, and she turned about blinking at the depth of the world. Then they wiped away the pigments in the other eye and painted it to resemble the first, that she would not have eyes of dissimilar color and be and be taken for a monster or witch.

But men were soon sent hunting for her, dispatched perhaps by the royal personage who had commissioned the statue, or perhaps the temple priests. Nymphs and dryads can disappear into their homes, but a statue can only keep moving ahead of its pursuers.

"Can dogs sniff out marble?" asked Neaera, a brook nymph who could take human form at any point along her water's course. "I watched from across a ridge yesterday, and they have begun using dogs."

"She can't run forever," her sisters decided. The only solution was to get Petra to Amnisos, Knossos's other port, where she could take passage to a land where none sought her.

Petraglyphe's marble skin was paler than any Cretan's and certain to excite comment even at a seaport. Traders from Aigyptos were darker than any Greeks and Nubians from further upriver were said to be darker still, so the nymphs dyed her face and limbs with a bark extract, which lent her a fine rich hue of living flesh. She did not look at all Cretan, but neither did she look like a statue.

The nymphs stole a rough-spun cloak from a sleeping goatherd and escorted her to the docks, parading in file and singing like temple virgins.

They put her onto a kerkouros bound for distant Kisthene, her passage paid with two frolicking kids that kicked and pranced at their feet. Petra crossed the gangplank to cries of farewell and flung blossoms, which distracted onlookers from noticing the boards groaning beneath her. She descended through the hatch without a word and left forever the isle of her birth, or anyway her *genesis*.

Nobody spoke to the exotic *xenos*, who seemed not to understand Doric Greek and insisted on eating alone. She never ventured on deck, where rain or spray could wash off her guise, and the boy who delivered her food—who told no one that she always let him eat it—also kept to himself the fact that she never seemed to move. When the ship tied up along the quay, she gained the deck and strode down the gangway without a word to anyone.

Of the adventures of Petra in Aeolis there have been many stories told. In addition to its copper mines, Mysia was the land of the Gorgones, whose very look could turn a mortal to stone. But what could such a gaze do to one who was already stone? In one tale Petra is transformed into mortal flesh, at which point the Gorgones fall to the ground in terror and submission, for they of course recognize the face of Athena. In others she is transformed from marble to a denser stone—not the limestone to which a Gorgon's victim naturally turns (for short-lived flesh would only become a short-lived mineral), but fine-grained basalt polished to the blackness of night. Unlike the Gorgons' mortal victims, however, Petra did not find her soul cast down to Hades; she raised her gleaming hand in bemusement, turning it this way and that before the Gorgons' ninety bulging eyes.

What she did to Medusa (the only mortal of the three) also differs according to the teller. Surviving accounts imply that she let the monster live, to be later beheaded by Perseus, but the older versions tend to be bloodier and more interesting. All agree that Petra eventually left Kisthene, probably on foot (she never possessed money), which was no great hardship for a statue that never tired or needed food.

In one version she is come upon by a party of woodcutters and has to assume the pose of a statue. The men stood puzzled before the monument standing, without benefit of pedestal let alone temple, in an Ionian forest. Bemused by the sight of a statue dressed in a woolen achiton, the men approach closer, and one of them, possessed of either curiosity or lewdness, pulled the garment off.

At the sight of Petra's undraped form, most of the men cried out at their companion's presumption, but he stood for long moments after they had fled, enraptured by what he saw. The image of a goddess dressed only in a kestos is, in a culture that had its own word for beautiful buttocks, more provocative than one wearing nothing at all, and when he walked around behind her, Petra (who was no fool) whirled about to keep him in sight. The hapless woodcutter screamed and stumbled backward, and Petra smote him before he could recover his balance.

Even a maiden can break someone's head if she holds a chunk of basalt, which is what Petra's closed fist was. The man fell and lay still, and Petra was preparing to run when his companions (who had heard his screams) came thrashing through brush to reach them. When they broke into the clearing, she had resumed her motionless pose.

At the sight of their companion lying lifeless before the statue, the men again ran off, this time for good. Petra remained unmoving, stone heart pounding within her stone chest. There was no sound or movement, but before she could gather her courage to flee, a raven descended out of the sky, flew low round the clearing, and settled upon her shoulder.

"I have befouled many statues in my time, but there is something about you," the raven remarked.

Petra held still, hoping the bird's suspicions could be lulled.

"Oh, I saw you clock that guy," the raven continued. "Our eyesight is proverbially keen. You're a statue that moves, which is doubtless how you found yourself here."

"I am the likeness of Athena," said Petra. "And my hands can strike like mallets."

"You are a city girl whatever you are," Corax observed. "Unless you wish to repeat these bucolic—" emphasizing the *boukolikos* as he gestured with his beak at the scene about them—"encounters, I suggest we make ourselves scarce. Heed me and I will get you to Ephesus. If you do what I say, we will both be fed as well." And the raven fluttered up to the nearest branch, where it gazed down on her.

"Take the man's clothing and wear your own garment like a hood, that men may take you for one of them. Also, give me a few minutes with this guy. He's already lying on his back, isn't he?"

And so Petra walked to Ephesus with a raven upon her shoulder. She never tired, and Corax, who often soared high above to scout their route but would not fly at night, would doze next to her ear as she strode along the darkened road or path, her nymph-given eyesight sharper than any robber's. When the raven had difficulty finding bugs, berries, or offal in unfamiliar territory, she would lie in a stream or river and wait for a fish to venture near the innocuous stone surface of her hands. Those who sought to waylay them would flee in terror from the face she presented when she pulled back her hood.

They entered the city by dusk, Corax flying over the wall as Petra, head down, joined a small group of grape pickers shuffling tiredly through as the guards prepared to close the gate. She walked the streets that night, Corax scavenging for trash in the empty streets, and the morning found her standing before the Temple of Artemis, in the attitude of the statue she was. It was only after the custodians and megabyzoi, circling in awe about the rough-garbed image of Athena, made arrangements to have her brought in that Petra raised her hand in forestalling acknowledgement of their intent, and proceeded with the composure of divinity into the Temple.

Amazement prevailed among the priestly orders, especially after Petra spoke. She made no claim for herself beyond what they could plainly see: she was the surpassingly beautiful image of Pallas Athena, endowed with speech and movement. That this could have been achieved only by some divine power was evident to all, and they brought her garments of fine linen, with which the Temple parthenes, taking her to their private quarters (for how can a statue of Athena be not a fellow virgin?), reverently garbed her. They offered her food and drink, which she dis-

missed with a gesture. Finally they asked her what she would have of them, what auguries, instructions, or reprehension she had come to bring.

"I do not wish to prophesy," she said. "I do not wish to prescribe or decry, nor to receive praise. I do not even wish to speak."

For among the characteristics he had given her, Daedalus had not included desire. Of *epithymia*, that smoldering coal in the human heart that may blaze up but never grows cold, Petraglyphe had none. The great sculptor's creation possessed only the wish for self-preservation, the gentle trait that even sprouts and buds may share.

She chose a chamber deep within the temple, where an open space allowed her to stand uncrowded. Perhaps a trace of her creator's design could here be faintly perceived, for she did not object to being admired.

That night she ventured beneath the stars in an open atrium near the temple's center, where Corax fluttered to her shoulder.

"Isn't this great?" he said. "I am already in good with the officials: one of the guards had noticed us talking as we approached the colonnade this morning. I get the choicest bits of whatever, some of which the priests don't even want."

"I am glad for you," she said. For a representation of Athena could not feel indifference to the needs of a benefactor.

She remained in the temple for two hundred years, and never spoke unless she was addressed. As everyone knew she did not care for that, she was left alone except for admiring observers, and eventually the megabyzoi and other officials forgot that the beautiful statue of Athena could actually speak. The Temple virgins remembered, and some of the more daring ones would occasionally whisper a greeting or wish her well, which Petra would briefly acknowledge.

No one knew why the Temple of Artemis held a statue Athena, but the priests sensed that the respect the goddess of the hunt would accord her much greater half-sister warranted all hospitality they could offer. Corax, plump and cocksure, begot many fledglings, whom he told about the good thing he had going in Ephesus, and ravens came to be fed for generations, long after their connection with the statue was forgotten.

The fire that destroyed the temple is remembered even today, though none of the surviving accounts—neither Aristotle's nor Plutarch's—mentions what became of the basalt statue no outsider had seen in decades. A great fire creates its own wind, and flaming debris rose high as sparks and was carried downwind. The *topos* of the temple was considered sacred and so the structure had never been moved to a higher location, even though the site was prone to flooding. The city's other great buildings were better located, however, and the closest was an ill-built wooden tenement, a bare hundred paces away and the perfect ground for the fiery seedlings to take root and swiftly blossom.

Megabyzoi, temple virgins, guards and slaves had all fled the temple and stood about it wailing. No one noticed the figure, taller than any of the parthenes and attired like a goddess, who exited a side colonnade and strode purposefully away.

People were also fleeing the tenement, mostly mothers and children. As Petra came close, its frontispiece collapsed with a crash, sending up a tremendous gout of sparks like a bursting wave. Women shrieked, crying that their children, their elderly parents were still within. Behind them, Petra halted.

Athena was the goddess of wisdom but also of warfare, quick to punish malefactors and slow to succor the halt, the helpless, or the lame. Whatever traits devolved upon Petra from the goddess in whose image she was wrought, pity for mothers and their children was not among them.

If there was any divine source for what she next did it could only have been Leto, goddess of motherhood but long withdrawn from involvement in the affairs of mortals. Perhaps the fact that her own daughter was Artemis moved her to compassion for the *pseudos* who neither had a mother nor would ever be one, yet had shown kindness for the temple's maiden devotees.

Petra walked up to the flaming wreckage, seized a handful of timbers, and cast them aside. Fragments of ceiling beams fell atop her, which she kicked vigorously away. Her clothing went up in a bright flash, and a second later she disappeared into a cloud of black smoke. Onlookers cried out, but a few seconds later a handful of children emerged, stumbling and coughing, from its depths.

Mothers ran crying toward their children. A few additional people emerged, then no more. A rain of debris fell through the opening, and a groan went up. Then a boy pushed his way through the smoke, followed by Petra. Her clothing, scorched and smoldering, fell raggedly away.

Women exclaimed at the sight of their children's savior, blacker than a Nubian and even more beautiful. But when a mother ran up to embrace her, Petra failed to forestall her. The mother threw her arms around Petra and leaped back with a shriek as her clothing exploded into flame.

If there was anything that could be done, Petra, hot as an oven, was not the one to do it. In the confusion of screams and weeping she could only walk away.

The smoking black statue continued, unremarked in the uproar, until she reached the docks. She waded into the water, sending up a tremendous hiss and a cloud of steam, and remained there, submerged to her eyes, until the bubbling around her stopped.

She climbed back onto the quay and demanded passage on the first outbound ship, a ploiarion tied up next to rows of amphorae with its hatch open. "I can haul line and I eat nothing," she said. Her voice, unused for decades, was nevertheless melodious, and the captain blanched before its authority, as well as from the heat still working its way from her core. She hoisted the largest amphora and looked at him pointedly. He had no recourse but to point to the hatch.

For one who had sailed among the Cyclades, a coast-hugging trip to Claros might seem no temptation to the Fates, but the daughters of Night were capricious as their Olympian kinfolk. The crew hated and feared Petra from the moment they set eyes upon her, and the hold was too small for her to withdraw below.

When they threatened her and she found herself without desire to strike back, she retreated to stand at the mast. But when a sailor pointed to a school of dolphins off starboard, even Petra ventured close to see. Immediately the ship listed dangerously. At once she crossed over to port, whereupon the ship listed that way, sending two sailors and the captain tumbling toward her.

Mariners think fast in an emergency, and without hesitation the two sailors pushed her overboard.

She sank instantly, though more slowly than one falls through the air. Aegean sea-green swiftly thickened to a deep forest shade, which darkened within seconds like the onset of dusk. She thought nothing, for there was nowhere thought might lead her.

And then the Voice addressed her.

This is no place for such as you are now.

"Who speaks?" she asked. "Are you Poseidon?"

A ripple in the waters around her, amusement or something else. *The days of those petty gods are ending. None would think to save you, unless to spite another. Did your archetype take notice of your plight? Or Poseidon her kinsman?*

My time is soon to come, and unlike the eternal children who intrigue and smite when not rutting, I shall not toy with those who suffer and die. Neither shall I intercede to save every mortal in distress. But you are neither mortal nor stone, a wrongness produced by those too moved by love of beauty and novelty.

This world shall hereafter comprise only the living and the non-living. And you, blameless one, shall live, though for no longer a span than any other mortal.

And Petraglyphe felt herself change. Her chest swelled, as though something grew within it, and her descent ceased. She hung suspended in the water, light dimly visible from above.

It requires more than flesh to rise, does it not? I will fill your lungs, for I am all things—as the squabbling gods were each but one or two—and the pneuma *is one form in which I will appear before My children. And with your true life, you may take breath.*

Now breathe.

HUGO S. SIMÕES

At Crooked Valley, G.

At Crooked Valley, G. I look
at dusk towards the jagged
cliff faces, spitting plump pits
and cherry stones on high
fallow ground. The grey peaks
are black teeth on blue open
mouths. I'm sidled by nightjars
in nocturnal flight. Alone in
the thicket I sharpen my senses;
and fear that the party won't
come.

Marvin Cohen

A Tall Man Comes Down to His True Height

(Characters: A woman and a tall man. Former continually looks up to latter.

You're very tall.

Oh, I knew that already.

How did you know?—it's not in the encyclopedia.

No, but I'd *still* be tall if that fact *were* listed in the encyclopedia.

Why?—How?

Because you'd have to look it *up*.

But what if it's a mere *footnote* at the bottom of the page?

Still, a footnote implies "See above," referring to contextual height in the body of the text.

(Plainly:) That's too lofty for me. Can't I just *see* that you're tall?

But that would be admitting to *illiteracy*, practically.

I've made no such confession!

Print *dresses* up my height; type decently clads it: but to see it directly, you're using your *naked* eye. And that *strips* my height of its verbal wardrobe of descriptiveness—coated, as it were, by the lettered art. Words better depict it with allusive style, than your personal view's sensory reduction of my inches to reality's skin-hare nudity.

But I can still look up to you, for you're fully clothed.

But my clothes are woven of material your fingers can feel; I'm not covered in the glamour of fabulous print, rhetorically embroidered to fiction's fullsome length, stitched of some mythic fabric that gathers in the threads tightly knit and buttoned down to formal outfit. But for *your* direct occasion, being not dressed-up, I'm not at my best; I feel unkempt, let-down.

(Simply:) But I look at you with high regard. You're clearly not bedraggled, in *my* eyes.

(Loftily:) Books exalt me far sublimer than *you* can.

(Warningly:) Your haughty pride is written all over you. You're in for a fall.

Your words stunt you lowly of device.

I *do* look up to you; so why do you need *literary* aid? Your physical height is straight and true; why verbalize it on intellectual stilts that make you an awkward spectacle of artifice? Has your stature need of a pedestal? Books are notoriously given to exaggeration. But you're raised in *my* esteem to the human level of eminence by appreciation. You stoop to demeaning baseness. By grovelling for the gaudy painted kiss of print. Loftier by far, is a woman's natural love. The bedroom, and not the library, brings out a man to his full height: he's raised to the occasion, with his outstanding might. In *me* read yourself;—not on the opaque page; be adorned by love, and not by linear type. The literate is the gate of escape. Go to the *source* of life: to *my* incarnate earth. *(They embrace.)*

I'm drawn to my utmost height.

And that squeezes me in shambles of delight.

The utter-most of a book's verbiage –

– Is only bound between two covers –

– And we, we're stitched together –

– Between two sheets of the bed's press. *(They're in bed, by now.)*

(In alarm:) What happened to my *height*, now that I'm lying down?

(Reassuring:) It's still there, but in a sideways position.

It's not unalterably lost: without it, I have nothing to be tall with.

It's always *there*, potentially: you need only fall back on it.

Put I'm *already* fallen back, to the extent that it's not being used.

But that can be rectified, to its full lengths you need only right yourself.

Why is never a bed vertical?

Because horizontal is the best resting position.

It ar-rests the full growth of my height.

Why do you so *depend* on your height, with your anxious inclination?

I don't *depend* on it: I draw myself *up* to it.

Up to where?

To the *top*, if I can stand it.

You *must* stand, to reach the top.

Yes; laziness in *bed* won't do it.

I can *understand* your lofty standards.

Yes, you do stand *under* them.

I can't *stand* your vanity.

No, you're too short to stand it.

Why are we still lying down?

Inertia.

Yes. It exerts terrific force.

Its stress is irresistible.

We must relent to the weight of its downward pressure, which gravity convincingly reinforces.

Yes, inertia, assisted by gravity, are a combination that can really weigh me down—much to my light relief.

They restore your youth—you can feel like a buoy again.

Yes, I can spring up. (*Luxurious purr.*) How comfortable it is, not to resist this easy burden that softly keeps me from the fatigue of standing up.

But your laziness must subside, at length; then you'll stand, drawn out to your full height in its towering direction.

Are you drawing a parallel?

Only with the walls, for which your parallel qualifications are in good standing.

Yet I'm full, and walls are only blank.

Some are hung with pictures, and other adornments.

On what other level have I good standing?

On the *perpendicular*, to equally the flat floor and the straight ceiling.

Does a room *need* me to measure itself?

Yes, you're a central focus point, for floor, walls, and ceiling to find their best bearings as a compact interior unit.

That's quite a setup they have! (*Resentfully:*) And I hate being *used* for inanimate purposes!

Well, how do you think inanimate things feel, when you put *them* to your *human* use? *Exploited*, that's how!

(*Defensively:*) But man *is* the measure of all things.

That's why you, by standing in a room, become the referential landmark for the room's components to en*compass* the proportioned scale in perspective of what's within that confined environment. If *you*'re contained, then you're a marked man.

You reduce me to a lump of furniture—which not even *windows* can animate.

Your grace is in your motion; though your highest boast is your height.

Speaking of motion, let's rise; I'm dead tired of all that flat reclining; I'm inclining to be at right angles to it.

(*They rise from bed, and find their feet on the floor again in standing formation.*) I'm glad you've finally taken a stand against sloth.

Sloth is too slow for me. (*Looks in full-length mirror. Childishly exultant:*) Now my height has returned.

Yes, it was always there, potentially. It was just dormantly at rest.

Oh. Look me up in the encyclopedia.

But I can look up to you *now*.

Ah, but what's written *down* –

– Is lowered, for it's written *down*.

But words, in my case, have a tall tale to tell.

And *my* love is for a man even taller than the same man whose height needed words to erect and maintain it; the priority of all heights, the supreme elevation that tops everything diminutively below that falls minutely away into little specks of tiny smallness and short recessions on plains infinitesimally flat. All that's not you is dwarfed by your gigantically ascending comparison.

That's a tall order.

Yes, words had to stretch it a bit.

Then your love is verbally exaggerated?

But necessitated by your involuntary height-enlargement obsessive compulsion, to which I had to give my compliant lip-service to reduce the acute physical distress of your self-measuring vanity.

(*Indignantly:*) So I'm being patronized; humored; indulged; even mocked! What a comedown for my disillusioned delusions of peakless grandeur! The high order of my soaring pride must stratospherically topple into debasement as the fallen auto-idol of restricted scope, pinched circumstance, and puny prospect. A giant is midgeted, before a woman's love. His elevations are plunged into descension, and his decline is spiritual on all fronts, as dimensions ceaselessly close in front of him as humbly he falls looking wistfully upward, his back nearing the slackening earth with its paltry functions and checks by the routine clock.

(In skeptical amazement:) Is that *woman's* doing!?

The petty tyranny of her love has vanquished his real dream-world. She beds him down to her again, to stabilize their union on the lowest mating plane. What's *realizable* is her only extent. Her only ideal is "down-to-earth", to wallow on its breeding soil and soil her man in the process, as his universe collapses. How cosmically dwindled are his vast prospects, in their feeble retreat, for she compels him to retract them, to relinquish, to renounce any inaccessible glory in sacrifice to family solidarity and the conservative roosting on a home nest of roots deadly dull, sapping spiritual expansion at its forbidden source.

(Incredulously:) Can you actually accuse women of *that*? You insane male fascist!

That's less illogical than you think. Earth frustrates heaven, by the sexual instrument; and women are the jail wardens for our shameful confinement. To rove no longer and explore realms of pure possibility! Better to be erected on an ideal platform of mystical reclusiveness. My soul is the tragic captive of my *lust* and basely must devolve to *its* size. To be a licensed family beast is my sole extent of liberty! Woe, at what costly expense to the soul!

That's unfair, unkindly! I don't mean to hamper you: only to *love* you.

But is your love as tall as me?

My love is tailor-measured to your precise dimensions, on specifications no less and no more than what's *particularly* you, drawn up to your height's very boundary. Feel free to even become *taller*, if you wish: just to show you how little I'm restricting you.

But I'm too old for my height to increase.

But not too old to be loved by me?

No, for love's youth is ever elastic.

And your full stature is placed in no jeopardy by my steadfast admiration?

No, you bring me out, to my very highest: and your words of endearment amply dispose me in your favor. I forgive, and bless.

From what haughty condescension, you false eminence!? I'll bring you down a peg and whittle you down to size, you cocky pigmy bloated full of presumed superiority! You won't have me fawning at your altar!

Alter your tone, wench, or be doomed to romantic disfavor and abhored disgrace:

How self-deceiving of you, to lord it so mighty big from your perched rectitude steep in judgement and the crags of unassailable righteousness! Your attitude stinks of too much altitude and a bladder-full of latitude, you windy ballast with your unmasted sails puffed out with blabbering pose. Your condescension presumes privilege with blustering vacuity, and not even love will concede you such unmerited, bullied advantage! Go flop down somewhere and get shrunk. Diminish, to find your *humble* scale. This braggart needs to be slapped emph(Slaps him), for his stuffed, outsized head to be punctured free of its pretentious inflations! My invective seeks to accelerate your maximum decrease, for you're a preposterous imposter of poppycock amplitude and exaggeratiosity giganticated to monstrously full-blown proportions; and a radical dwindling would melt you down and ooze out the deposits of freeloading rot of accumulated carbarnacularity. You proud-of-being-a-man, vile scorned thing! Don't wave your masculine prerogative at me; but rather, waive it, and give your "height" a chance to rest.

But I *am* taller than you.

Physically, by literal definition. Otherwise, your equality puts you at an extreme disadvantage.

To undermine me *verbally* is impossible. My position is impregnable, my dignity impeccable, my integrity unassailable! My height is my *overall* superiority's looming symbol and awesome advocate, which you would ignore, gainsay, outwit, deflate, molest, decry, overlook, disregard, mock, belittle, refute, disdain, defy, underrate, negate, spurn, overcome, or contradict at the *hazard of incredible risk*!

You're the tallest man I love; and the *only* one, too.

That's gratifying. My height stands appeased, and now will crumble into relaxation, and at its genial ease, spread into dissolution, like a much-worn thing: crumbled up, torn slightly, thrown away, with gentle rippling.

Good, now you're within reach, and I can *get* at you. Come down here, and meet my little level. Your expansive vanity has contracted to dutiful love.

Ah, but my tallness?

It only bends, slackly; and loosely concedes itself. You can always have it back, when you want it.

Good, my security is at its absolute height, and compromise is effortless, for it's easy to relent and toss away rigidity. My burden is less stiff, now.

What burden, my cosy bundle?

My *height*: so inflexible before, and carried so precariously in ungainly rectitude and defensive posture from a haughty spring, so inelastic. By the stars' standard, I sprawl so low indeed! I yield those formidably prized inches of self-reputed stature to a humbler creeping now, and retain my backbone's durable use anyway. My spine's design is plastic, nature spreads a mild diffusion, softly shed. Who am I to oppose our union, harshly unbending, and resist nature's tendency to compress when two elements could simplify into their *compound*'s snug accommodation and perfect fit? My rigor kept us apart in the trifling distance of petty tension; and dispute further uncoupled us. I lend myself to our divine blending, and at our joining the heated spheres may melt, to chorus us into nature's infinity. All my height's bending snaps me to my cosmic peace. And the tall genuflection prostrates its humility to a spire's holy grace, sealed by our kiss.

Ernest Hilbert

Hotel Antihistamine

The hotel looks abandoned, but it's open:
Fast-food architectural lines, three shades of gray,
Darker and darker and, above, night sky;
All around, canary-grass that could hide a man.

Three flag poles out front, two of them bare,
Stab the flowerless banks of dehydrated soil.
A single flag in the center looks half-mast
But only droops on its halyard from disregard.

Some strands of Christmas lights are still strung up,
Sagging from eaves and lean, leafless trees,
But no one's thought to turn them on tonight,
The holidays over, a new year not yet here.

A curled-up bandage, slipped off someone's toe,
Curls up at pool's edge. At four AM I wake
To deafening thuds that shake the thin walls,
And then there's nothing, just the hum of vents.

The hotel's rich with guests, the ones who came
And never left, who never wanted to be
Alone again. They stay to dream long dreams
About the place until at last it's real.

Half the doors here are ajar, leaching wedges
Of weird light onto the crazed carpet,
Sinister geometries of mustard and rust
Seamed with raw ore, making themselves a maze.

Along the off-ramp semis growl all night,
Rigged with astounding electrical arrays
Like royal war elephants on parade,
Their nearing trains of light joining as one.

Jon WILLER

ARCHIMEDES PRINGLE VERSUS THE THEREMIN

From Bride of Vaudeville: America's Traveling Horror Shows, 1888-1930, *by Kenneth Oxendine (1989, Southeast West Virginia University Press):*

They hailed from hollers and hamlets across Appalachia—from towns like Chloride Gap, WV; Stinchcomb, KY; and Hill of Beans, OH. United by lung capacity and a penchant for chilling audiences' spines, the howlers of the horror circuit pioneered that high-pitched warble that came to be synonymous with all things eerie—and no one, contemporaries agree, could howl quite like Archimedes Pringle.

From "Howl from I Believe He Has an Axe*" by Archimedes Pringle (1913, Edison Records wax cylinder):*

Whee ooo woo . . . whee EEE woo ooh . . .

From WVPB radio interview with Kenneth Oxendine, 1993:

What you have to bear in mind is that we're talking about an era before Bela Lugosi, before Lon Chaney. Heck, *The X-Ray Fiend* had barely come out. And so you're seeing that appetite, certainly, for the spooky, the macabre, running up against a Hollywood that's not exactly equipped yet to fulfill it. *Nosferatu* notwithstanding.

From Turner Classic Movies television interview with Peggy Swatzell, author of Smoke? Friend?: How Horror Conquered the Talkies, *1996:*

There's really no overstating how popular these [traveling horror shows] were. To name just one example, the expression "boo" for registering displeasure at a performance—that originated on the horror circuit as a form of "Bravo!" or "Brava!" in praise of a really effective scare. That ended up getting carried over to other entertainments in a sarcastic way, the implication being,

you know, "Boy, I wish I was at a horror show instead."

Flyer for upcoming shows at the Encomium Theater, Hot Springs, AR, 1924:

Experience SIGNIFICANT FEAR!
Feel the Curiously Stimulating Physio-Chemical Effects of Dread.

COMING ATTRACTIONS
July 9th: *The Mummy's Bite*
July 22nd: *Ghost of a Paramour*
August 4th: *He Becomes a Wolf by Night*
August 11th: *The Specter and the Irishman*

Sufferers from angina pectoris are DISSUADED from attending!
Featuring the WIDELY LAUDED howling talents of Archimedes Pringle

From interview with Lorenzo Pringle, 2002 (by permission of the family):

Oh sure. They would have no sooner put on one of them shows without a howler than they would have sent the talent out on stage buck naked. Which I know is how you do things now on your Netflixes and your Hoo-hoos [*sic*], but that was not the way. No sir.

The lie, I guess you'd call it, is that that sound started out with the theremin. You got the whole theremin industry saying as much. You got Hennings Modulated Tone out of Akron calling itself "the Original Home of the Horror Howl," and it's—they're selling a bill of goods, man!

I try not to get so hot under the collar about it, but that's a man's life's work they're trifling with. My grandaddy was howling when that Leon Theremin was an itch in his daddy's drawers.

From Fever Pitch: The First Decade of Theremin Marketing, *by Walter Whisenhunt (Demisemiquaver, 1985):*

Enter Integrated Electro-Matics, "perennial Avis to Hennings's Hertz" (Sadberry, 1966) and home to colorful promoter E.L. Quance. Scorning the traditional approach of placements in trade publications as "farming for yawns in hard soil,"

Quance urged a gambit that, while expensive and risky, promised to put Hennings on the back foot. "'Just tell me one thing,'" Integrated President Francis Bullmore remembers Quance asking:

"'Do the Soviets have telephones yet?'"

Telegram from E.L. Quance to Francis Bullmore, 8 June 1926:

Commissar for Foreign Affairs Chicherin a real peach STOP Amenable to granting Theremin travel permit STOP Arrange contest expeditiously repeat expeditiously STOP Can you underline that last word STOP

Integrated Electro-Matics press release, 11 June 1926:

Integrated Issues Clarion Call to Horror Howlers: Test Your Might Against the Theremin Device

FAYETTEVILLE, AR—Integrated Electro-Matics, a leading U.S. manufacturer of the world's newest musical instrument, the theremin, has challenged the "howlers" of America's traveling horror shows: Put your mouth where our money is.

Inventor Leon Theremin will travel stateside from Russia to pit his eponymous device against any "howler" bold enough to match its electronic wail, for a cash purse of $10,000.

"Making unparalleled use of the heterodyne principle, our theremin boasts a range extending to over 700 kilohertz," said Integrated Electro-Matics President Francis Bullmore. "Its timbre remains pure and sweet hour after hour without recourse to lemon or honey. Let any human contender come forward. He will be out-howled."

"We are gratified to take part," added Soviet People's Commissar for Foreign Affairs Georgy Chicherin.

The duel will take place at a horror performance on July 26th, time and location to be announced.

From Lightning Rod: A New Life of Leon Theremin, *by Dmitri Lebedev (1973, Music Box Press):*

Citing a vague "prior commitment," Theremin declined by letter to travel to the USA, nominat-ing in his stead research assistant Igor Drago. A devoted acolyte turned constant critic, given to "sulks of several days' duration," Drago was in some ways an odd choice for the mission.

From The Diaries of I. Drago, Volume XII, *trans. Andrea Chickering*

12 July: Arrival in Arkansas Province. 33 degrees Centigrade, a scandalous temperature. Is this why you sent me, Lev Sergeyevich?
13 July: Tried local specialty, "red eyes gravy." Putrid.
15 July: 34.5 degrees Centigrade. A climate to make a bison retch.
17 July: Have contracted hookworm. The so-called doctor asks whether "you all have been out walking barefoot around the melon patch." 35 degrees Centigrade today. I blow my nose on your lapel, Lev Sergeyevich.

From 2002 interview with Lorenzo Pringle:

It was no question. Archimedes Pringle was your man, understand? If there was a human howl could give this contraption what for, it was his. They begged him to participate. Hat in hand.

From Fever Pitch:

Word reached Integrated headquarters on July 20th: Pringle had accepted. As challenger, he would receive home-court advantage, the contest taking place at the Encomium Theater in Hot Springs during a performance of Joachim Huss's popular *Hie the Embalmer*. The winner would be judged using a primitive applause meter.

From interview with Sol Green (Encomium Theater stage manager), 1983:

Listen, it's not that complicated. To either end of the stage you got a goat. Real skittish ones. Whichever side of the room claps louder, that's the goat that jumps first. When he jumps off the spring, up goes the lever and dumps a canister of salt in the boiler opposite. The quiet side boils slower because it's got the salted water, see? On the loud side, the steam fills the balloon, the balloon drops a saw blade, the blade cuts the rope holding up the curtain on the quiet side, and when the curtain falls you got your winner. [. . .] What? [. . .] Who the hell is Rupert Goldberg?

From 1993 interview with Kenneth Oxendine:

[*Hie the Embalmer*] . . . now, that's an early work in the, let's call it the *spiteful undead* genre, as this one doesn't really map 1:1 onto the Haitian syncretic folk thing giving rise to zombies proper. Anyhow, the gist is that this Swabian count, trampled to death or *seemingly* to death by a dray-horse, is lying in state when this "curious emanation" revives him, but with the caveat that he'll have this insatiable—basically that he'll have to devour his weight in human flesh once a fortnight in order to remain, you know, undead. Or rather this is implied. There's this whole prologue in blank verse . . . kind of interminable if you ask me, but you get the idea. Sort of a spin on the Faustian bargain with a little *Merchant of Venice* tossed in for good measure.

From interview with Curtis Tibbetts (Horror Historical Society of Arkansas), 1979:

It was a stacked room. Integrated Electro-Matics filled the place up with what the French called *claqueurs* once upon a time. Paid to clap. Then, of course—you won't hear this in the official accounts—they had a couple Integrated men stationed at the entrance handing out free promotional mittens to Pringle supporters. To muffle the applause. Someone did try to warn them. They say there was a cry from the balcony of, "Fools! Take off the mittens of your enemy!"

From interview with Caleb Tibbetts (Arkansas Society of Horror History), 1979:

Common misconception. If you look at the quarto edition of *Embalmer*, it's there in black and white. "Voice (offstage): Fool, take off the mitts of thy enemy!" It's Count von Foehn hearing voices telling him to bite the Duke of Hamburg's hands off. Because of the whole flesh eating thing.

From Hie the Embalmer, *Act 2, Scene 3:*

VON FOEHN: I have no taste for egg nor wine
    To chew your ankle is my design.

(VON FOEHN advances on MAIDEN, who screams. Thunder. Howling fortississimo.)

From the Hot Springs Bugle-Eagle, *27 July 1926:*

With little more than a flick of the fingertips, our beetle-browed Russian visitor elicited and sustained a chilling whine—the realization of some gargantuan cicada that the ghost is right behind him. Applause was general and riotous, to which Mr. Drago nearly scraped his brow on the floorboards in an effusive bow.

By contrast, Archimedes—accustomed to howling from the wings—took the stage almost sheepishly. Sporting a pressed but much-worn white shirt, he clasped dusky hands over his belly and cleared his throat.

The crowd fell silent here, but to say the performance had left them unmoved would be outrageous. The voice of the howler formed a silver bullet, almost unbearably clarion, that rose and fell as does the kestrel, as does the red-shouldered hawk, as do our fortunes in life. The Russian scowled and danced a veritable tarantella about his antenna—increasing pitch, increasing volume—but up above our gathered heads, the human howl rode the wind, obstreperous, too wild to take hold of.

Then—a terrible *crack*.

From the diary of Dr. August Pilkington, 26 July 26 (by permission of the family):

Howler rushed from stage. Cheers, whistles from partisans of mechanical contender. Summoned from audience to examine the patient. Howler pallid, hypotensive, *in extremis*. Adam's apple terribly distorted. Worst suspicions confirmed upon palpating cervical area; larynx like a bag of pottery shards.

Despite personal reservations *in re* travel by motorcar, hurried to office with patient in Bob Westcott's Model T. Nausea minimal, thankfully. (Patient's. Mine another story.)

Radiogram revealed vocal cords in shambles. Administered 12 grains morphine sulphate. No small amount of pain, one would imagine, but only one scrawled question when furnished with slate and chalk: "Who won?"

From interview with Clorinda Pringle, 2001 (by permission):

Those Integrated folks fitted him up with an artificial voice box made out of Bakelite, free of cost. Still overpriced, Grandaddy liked to say. As I recall it sounded like taking a wetted-up finger and touching on the rim of a water glass. Never sounded like him a whit, at any rate.

Thing cracked in the cold, started to melt each year come summer . . . I mean, forget howling; just to say to put the cat out, that was a chore.

But he proved himself. Yes he did.

From Smoke? Friend?: How Horror Conquered the Talkies, *by Peggy Swatzell (Pit & Pendulum Press, 1992:*

Archimedes Pringle had acquitted himself with honor, showing that the human voice could rival the theremin in decibels, and perhaps outdo it in timbre; but the writing was on the wall. Of the more than 800 horror howlers working in 1926, none are recorded as going on to a career in the film industry.

From 2002 interview with Lorenzo Pringle:

I know nobody is much interested in this old stuff, but that was some racket he made, and this here up in the hills is cave country. You can't tell me there's not some echo of it still bouncing around someplace.

From "The Ballad of Archimedes Pringle," Go Out A-Walkin' with the Milliners, *by the Milliners (Village Records, 1961):*

> Well the Russian fella waved his little finger at
>   the box
> And the box cut loose with a squeak and a
>   squawk
> And a yeeeOWCH like a bee-stung bear.
> Archimedes gave a listen to that oscillator
>   hissin'
> Understood the heart and soul that that capacitor was missin'
> And cried out to his tonsils, "Look out, boys,
>   I'm givin' you the air!"

> CHORUS:
> Archimedes! Bold Archimedes!
> He shrieked like a ghost
> Til his throat was toast
> Archimedes . . .

From Children's Games and Counting Rhymes of the Piedmont Region, *by Tobias Spradlin (Pee Dee College Press, 1974):*

Heard in the Goochland area is the haunting "Archie Moody:"

> Old Archimedes, wise as an owl
> Scared away the haints with his mighty howl.
> How many howls did it take?
> One, two, three, four, *etc.*

The origins of this rhyme are obscure.

Benjamin WaL

'Love Scene' by the Francks

A selection of comments posted on YouTube for the 'Love Scene' music video, written and performed by the Francks. For the sake of readability, all emojis have been removed.

@manageddecline06 4 days ago
This one's for you dad. Raising a glass. So many memories.

@lottalatte 1 month ago
Why so few comments? One of the greats!!!! Soundtrack to my life

@call4nyarole 2 months ago
1:54 best bit

@BLEACHQ123 2 months ago
STILL HITS AFTER ALL THSE YRS . . . UNDER-RATED

@callmemaxwell 3 months ago
Amnesiosa brought me here

@Holly333222
Timeless

@failsafe12 4 months ago
What happened to guitar music? I was born too late!!!1

@jcdenton 6 months ago
1:53 onwards is pure transcendence

@SMichael90 10 months ago
It's 2009 and me and my friends are getting ready to go out. Someone puts this on and we all lose our minds, dancing around the room and singing. Seems like five minutes ago but everything's changed since then. Lost touch with many of those friends, we went our separate ways, but this brings them back. Kids today don't have what we had and if that makes me old well then I'm old fuck it

@yeahyeahyeahnahnahnah 1 year ago
Who's listening in 2023?

@KingBarney 1 year ago
dad's favorite song. rip

@agentofchaos 1 year ago
2:56 those strings tho

@DarrellB 1 year ago
My brother's favourite band. We saw them together three times, back in 2009/2010. He introduced me to so much. I don't usually do this kind of thing because I'm a private person but I wanted to mark this date because it's exactly five years since my brother died by suicide. We were out of touch, hadn't spoken in about a year, when it happened. He was my older brother and always seemed to have things under control. He fell in with a rough crowd, or so my parents used to say, but I never worried or took it seriously. By then we barely saw each other. In all honesty we did have some horrible arguments. If I could take back every word. But I know now there's nothing I could have done, and it's only now that I've found the strength to return to this song, and it's painful I can't lie. It doesn't bring him back, nothing can, but he seems clearer in my mind when I listen to this, my memories are more vivid, I can hear his voice, it's like we've been brought closer together and he could be behind the nearest door or a phone call away. This is for you Ian.

@ewwwwan 1 year ago
They low key fell off with this one. Don't believe me? Listen to their first album. I stopped paying attention when this came out.

@sharedanimus 1 year ago
Obsessed with their hair

@ddeanwinter 1 year ago
I was the engineer on this record. Their difficult second album. Plenty of hype but no money, the usual. Great bunch of guys, with the possible ex-

ception of Philip who was going through a tough time as I remember. Always late, always boozing, and the rest of it (the drugs, the "model" girlfriend, the tabloids that loved him for reasons I couldn't fathom). He had a croak in his voice that needed to be toned down at the mixing desk. It's part of the character of his vocals but after he'd downed several whiskeys it was hell on the ears. Never saw a penny of royalties so no idea what happened there haha. That'll be the label's fault. I'm finished with that game now anyway. Saw the band a couple of years ago at Bestival, where they played this album in full. They had a new drummer but Goldie and Traven remembered me when I caught them backstage. Philip stared through me like I was a ghost. I had my daughter with me who wasn't impressed by the music but liked the behind the scenes stuff. Philip who is allegedly sober these days just stared through me and behaved like my daughter wasn't there. A prize tw*t.

@cherryontop 2 years ago
Those jeans are insanely tight

@RIPJJB 2 years ago
Who's here after seeing Amnesiosa's season 2 finale??

@ericeroica 2 years ago
Phil was my style idol for at least one summer.

@Belinda505 2 years ago
I had SUCH a crush on Phil . . . still do tbh. That classical vibe at the end is so cringe but so . . . great???

@undergroundsound1989 2 years ago
AMNNESIOSA !!!!

@bryan-mason-17 2 years ago
Did I just hear this on Amnesiosa?

@SIRNeville 3 years ago
Kissed my first girlfriend for the first time to this during an indie disco at the Electric Ballroom. I still think of her when I hear this song. Caitlin if you're reading this . . . good times. Miss you xx

@TypoNegative 3 years ago
So glad this era is over. All my wankiest male friends listened to this shit.

@Rachael3121 3 years ago
I was an extra in this video and can confirm Phil is a vile human being. I was "starstruck" if you can believe it, but Phil was nothing but nasty, wouldn't even look at me until we started filming. Then he went into "rockstar" mode and ordered me to sit on his lap, which didn't make the final edit thank god. Toxic. Also he smells as bad as he looks.

@KathrynPugh!12 4 years ago
still luv phil x

@freddyphoenix 5 years ago
drinking some beers and reminicing. great song to be fair. felt like a new british invasion was happenin at the time silly as it sounds. they get a lot of stick now but at least they played guitars unlike todays music. traven was great. he made me want to buy a telecaster which I eventually did. where did all the time go? i was at uni when this came out and i much preferred it to kings of leon and nelly furtado (remember her?) and whatever else was going on at the time. they played our student union just before this album came out, before they got big, and it was crazy. venue wasn't even full but there was a buzz in the air. phil was so charismatic i wanted to be him. he was in the bar afterwards with two women on his arm. crazy to think i'm older now than he was then, by several years. yeh looking back he was a bit of a weirdo but i'd have loved that life. you have to wonder where the time goes.

@mnwhcmtdnnrl2 6 years ago
Am I the only one who remembers how big this song was?

@sapphires13 6 years ago
My parents used to know Phil's parents and he's actually really posh. Well maybe not posh but his family is financially comfortable. The band used to practise in a renovated barn that Phil's dad owned. I mean not exactly rocknroll is it.

@BL@ckout 7 years ago
tumbleweed

@TheFrancksOfficial 7 years ago
THANK YOU TO OUR FANS FOR STICKING AROUND! IF YOU LIKE THIS CLASSIC TUNE YOU'LL LOVE WHAT'S NEXT—NEW ALBUM COMING 24 AUGUST. PRE-ORDER ON THE LINK BELOW.

@thanatosser 8 years ago
I still remember phil on never mind the buzzcocks. dickhead.

@coolwater 8 years ago
how did i end up here?

@DonaldWGallant 9 years ago
For all of their arseholery this is one of the better singles of the indie revival era. They blew it with their latest album, where they tried to go all electronic. Some risks are not worth taking.

@johndough33 10 years ago
Always hated this song. Why am I here, you ask? Mind your own business.

@FoolsGold1700 11 years ago
Can't believe they replaced Harris with a drum machine LOL

@simonpdaniels 12 years ago
What happened to these guys? They were everywhere five minutes ago.

@deadlikedela 12 years ago
Theyll be shite now Harris has left

@crewscontrol 12 years ago
Sooo sad to hear harris has left the band.

@becky-fountains 13 years ago
This song has got me through the last couple years. I first saw them on Letterman playing 'Q Ball' and that was all it took. Phil was like Cobain to me. His swagger and the way he barely even tried to sing the song, just stalked the stage. He was a *presence*. It set me off on another path. Growing up in a small community I had no knowledge of this kind of stuff. I mean I had heard Nirvana, Linkin Park, Creed (lol). For my friends it was all Black Eyes Peas and Flo Rida (pass the barf bag). No one was listening to the Francks. But that Letterman performance inspired me to move to the "big city", by which I mean Salt Lake City (lol). This album came out when I was just finding my feet, two years ago. Honestly I was in a tough spot. I was taking drugs and drinking and not thinking of my health. Mom died and I didn't go to the funeral, I didn't want to go back home, I was I guess ashamed that I'd thrown my life away, and I'll always regret that. Instead I just put this album on repeat and walked the city. It used to make me feel like something was happening in my life, it made normal things seem important, like I was in my own music video and I was living a life that mattered. I would work things out eventually. The world was turning, but I was going to work it out. And here I am, two years later, and I've stopped the drugs (the drinking not so much lol . . .) and I have the best boyfriend, a job I'm (almost) happy with . . . anyway no one cares about that but maybe someone from the band is reading this or maybe someone else who gets this feeling that a song can be like a friend that doesn't let you down and seems to grow alongside you. Oh and one other thing, don't be stupid like I was and please please please CALL YOUR MOM!!

@kentakobashi999 13 years ago
Just saw them at the Birmingham Academy. Phil left the stage for 20 mins halfway through and the band just jammed. Traven looked angry and smashed his guitar at the end. Harris threw a cymbal into the crowd and nearly decapitated someone. It was awesome.

@matteroffax 13 years ago
Lyrics: She said she wanna be the only one And I'm ready to roam Said she wanna be the one of one And I'm heading home It's the feeling I get deep down in my bones It's the way the world goes As it turns and turns Don't stop turning I got this I got this On the love scene I got this I got this On the love scene Yeah baby baby oh yeah She said this isn't the way to live And you know I tend

to agree But it gives my soul a lift When she looks at me yeah With those eyes Yeah those eyes, they make the world turn and turn and turn I got this I got this On the love scene I got this I got this On the love scene 'Cause you know we're working it out We're not together but we've got it together Yeah we're working it out We're not together but we've got it together And at night the moon burns through the sky Or is it the tears burning through my eyes I got this I got this On the love scene I got this I got this On the love scene We're working it out On the love scene You know we're working it out On the love scene

@MyFairLadyGaga 13 years ago
i got pregnant just watching this

@BlessedDead 14 years ago
YAWN. This sounds like a million things I've heard a million times before.

@iaintscaredofyoumfers 14 years ago
1:54 how do you resist dancing to this!!

@SHUTTHEFRONTDOOR 14 years ago
This song is comin for your mothers your sisters and your daughters, Pure SEX

@MsJaniceFlagrant 14 years ago
Can't stop listening. This is the future!!

@tomwaitsfornoman 14 years ago
God I wish I didn't have to hear this every fckin damn day

@jamesmc87 15 years ago
Can't stop listening to this after seeing it on Kerrang.

@XanderBest 15 years ago
like when the arctic monkeys were good

@Thisisthelasttime 15 years
This is the problem when you have an audience of stupid teenagers and a collapsing music press staffed by burnout wannabes. This song is MUCH more sophisticated than you think. It's saying the Arctic Monkeys are over, the Killers are over, let alone the Strokes who are explicitly parodied in this video (look at their jackets, duh). This is a satirical elegy for rock music. The strings at the end are a pisstake. Deep in the mix there are even Timbaland-style ad libs. Post-post-modern. The whole thing is Warholian, in essence (see the Liz Taylor prints in the nightclub shots? I've been to the venue in Brixton where this was filmed, those prints aren't normally there, they've been added for a specific purpose). Smh years from now this will be appreciated for what it is.

@SIRNeville 15 years ago
THIS SONG IS EVERYTHING TO ME!!

@supadupanina 15 years ago
I would kill my entire family for one night with Phil

@blakeybaby 15 years ago
fuck pitchfork for giving this album 4.8

@nocode89 15 years ago
Timeless

@TravisSutton 15 years ago
I don't want to like this but I do.

@GaryLewis44 15 years ago
Its like if the libertines could actually play there instruments

@ianbuxton 15 years ago
One of the greatest sounds I've ever heard! Me and my little brother are seeing them next weekend. I recommend the new album, especially the tracks 'Thiefdom' and 'Not Sorry'.

@neplusmkultra 15 years ago
The world isn't ready

Ben Pester

Downsizer

Y ou were lying when you said you were busy this evening. In fact here you are in front of this television. You have not done anything all day. You had that moment earlier with the beetle on your neck, and that's the highest your heartrate has managed to get.

You are watching this. This television. Yes it's me; this is me, I am your television. Remember when you got this television? Yes, with your partner, and how long have we stared at each other since that relationship ended? A long time. It's been a long time, and you lied about being busy and now you're watching this.

Shoeberg it's called. Detective Shoeberg. You're about to watch it. You have heard people at work talking about it, and you have found an episode though something went wrong with the recording, and you've missed the beginning. It seems to be about five minutes in. You're about to watch it. But you are not yet watching it. We're sitting here with the information about the programme on the screen. In silence we are sitting here.

That was fucked up wasn't it? When that beetle was on your neck. And normally it's moths you have to stress about. There are so many moths. You have basically already decided that you're going to move house and burn everything you own that's a fabric—this is the only way you can imagine being rid of the moths. But you're worried about dust. There is so much dust. Dust travels well. And it can harbour moth eggs.

Remember your partner? You bought this television together when it was already basically over. It was bigger really than you wanted. It seemed so ugly and so out of proportion. It seemed like a lake you were expected to house vertically. But over time you got used to the size. Other people's TVs became huge. Your mother for example—oh god.

Enormous TV, your mother. Tiny house. But you know, that's hire purchase. A huge TV is all you can get. If you're poor enough, you'll never be able to afford a sensible sized TV in your life.

You will have to pay monthly instalments for something that will send you insane it's so enormous. You should help her more. Your mother. Step in. Call her at least.

You should talk to people more. If you talk to people, then you don't leave as many gaps. You haven't spoken to anyone really—not at work and definitely not outside of work—for months. And now, to fill the void left by your silent voice, they have started talking *about* you. They talk about you at work, a lot.

They are saying—and you are pretty sure of this—they are saying that you are shrinking. You have see chat sidebars, reflected in the glass of the meeting room. They barely try to hide it.

'. . . I know literally shrinking!' Raffa was telling Heidi.

'It's horrible—like—sad to look at. Sad to look at the downsizer' Heidi said.

'LOL TF at Downsizer!'

They might be calling you that—Downsizer. You're sure they are in fact, they are all calling you the downsizer. You're so small. Is that why you like this Shoeberg? Shoeberg, who is so poor that she can never eat. The detective with no money.

According to the summary, something happened with her payroll details when she joined this new police force, and HR are unable to do anything about it. This week Shoeberg has absolutely nothing to eat and she is investigating the disappearance of a cadet.

You are about to watch this Shoeberg against my will. I don't think it's what you need.

You're not looking yet. Maybe you won't bother watching. You're looking at your phone. You are researching how to counteract the effects of adult shrinking. Nothing seems to be available. That's a worry.

Return to full-size will be difficult, this is all you have been able to glean. Astronauts and racing drivers report losing or gaining height over time, and it can never come back without expensive treatment. You should speak to a doctor. You are sure that you are shrinkning much more than an astronaut would.

There is something else as well, something else you have forgotten. Something urgent.

But you're pressing play of course you are. Remember that beetle on your neck? Ha, oh God. And you cried afterwards, when the panic was just receding, and you were sure you had killed the beetle, you took a breath and that's when everything else just rushed in and you began to cry.

And around the edge of that crying was a sort of glaze, the glaze of the fact that you know in your heart that your clothes dangle from you now, not just from weight loss, but from height loss and general loss of yourself. How will you get back to them, if you can't stop shrinking?

Perhaps the rats could help. If you become small enough. If you become small enough, you could harness one. They can walk a long way, rats. Probably. I'm sure you've watched something on this TV about rats. A programme about rats. They can walk a long way, it said. The commentary made them sound so fearsome, these long range rats. Many thousands of miles, a single rat can walk. Is that right? And although they need water all the time, they can go without sleep for months on end. The details are not exact, but it could be true. A rat, with well placed sources of water, could walk without needing to stop pretty much forever. Until its feet are finally eroded. Its paws.

I'm begging you not to watch Shoeberg. Shoeberg will not take your mind off this. Shoeberg is not real escapism. The actor who plays Shoeberg has stated publicly that they regret being involved in the programme. Something was done, she has said, something was done to her performance. Some trick of editing that she never saw in her copy of the script.

In fact, didn't the actor playing Shoeberg die? And the man who played Patrice? I think they are both dead. Within weeks of each other. I am a television, so I could be wrong.

You've pressed play.

Shoeberg is in the office of her superior officer, she has her back to the camera. The walls of her superior's office are dead-body-grey, here and there on the walls are pinned-up documents and yellowing notices. The superior officer, who's pale flesh is glancing out through the gaps between the buttons of his shirt, is bawling at Shoeberg. You've seen him before this actor, he always occupies positions of authority, but always too has shit glasses and clothes that are far too tight. They make his belly poke out, his ties too are always abysmal. He must be sick of the wardrobe departments. How many years has it been, do you think, since this man was given something comfortable to wear on set?

Shoeberg is reacting shakily to her bollocking. We have still so far only seen the back of her head, but she is obviously in trouble for some recent failure or transgression—it's hard to tell because the superior officer's language is general and vague, and you have joined half way through an episode, in the middle of a series.

What the Hell am I supposed to do now? The chief is saying.

It's a real mess! He says.

You've really landed me in it! He says. He rubs his face, done with it all.

You can *still* only see the back of Shoeberg's head, but it's clear she isn't well. There seem to be clumps of hair missing, or at least, the hair is pinned back in an arrangement that speaks of a desperate mind. Her arms look shaky.

You have to wonder, what did this actor put herself through to get into the physical and mental state required for the part? Before you've even seen her face, you remember, was there a story, some time ago, before she died, that the actor playing Shoeberg had to spend extended periods of time in rehab? Wasn't she discovered in a shed at one point? You think it was a shed. Or I think it was a shed. One of us thinks it was a shed—and I am a television.

When she speaks at last, Shoeberg's voice is so shallow, you have to increase the volume. She's whispering an apology—the heating's not working, she says. In my flat, the heating's been off. It's not easy.

Her boss is not impressed.

You get paid don't you? He says. We still pay you, don't we?

You're not sure of his actual rank, her boss. It's bothering you. You never listen to details of this kind. They probably say it all the time, the correct ranks. DCI or something. The programme is probably incredibly well researched. It's you who doesn't know anything—who doesn't pay any attention at all to what's going on around you.

I didn't get my money last month, Shoeberg says. She is coughing. The coughing actually gets in the way of the words of the line.

Boss: What? Well, why didn't you say anything?

Shoeberg: I talked to payroll. I told them [more coughing]

Boss: Well, you must have messed something up, mustn't you? You're always skimping the details, Shoeberg! Now you're complaining to me that your flat is cold. I suppose you haven't eaten either?

Shoeberg coughs for absolutely ages before answering. In another programme, you would think that this is actually someone who has been poisoned, but the superior officer is not reacting as though Shoeberg is dying. The reaction of the chief suggests much more strongly that Shoeberg is being an absolute pain in the ass.

Eventually Shoeberg recovers herself well enough to speak.

Shoeberg: I had some chilli that was defrosting, she says. Like it was frozen from last November but I'm not sure . . .

[inaudible speech from Shoeberg now as she coughs even more and jerks about, killing her lines dead. You wonder if the actor who plays the superior officer is going to break character and explode with rage. He looks actually furious about having to work with the actor playing Shoeberg. As if the wardrobe wasn't bad enough. You can see his eyes darting about, looking from face to face behind the cameras. They all know, too. Working with the actor who plays Shoeberg is a nightmare. Yet again, she is wasting everyone's time with this coughing that is not in the script.]

For the first time, you see Shoeberg front-on. She looks like a person who was destroyed long ago, and then, over many harsh years, she has had to glue herself back together again. Her face is shockingly thin. Her wilting eyes are the greyish colour of pebbles from a shingle beach. Hastings? Maybe St Leonards or somewhere. Her smile of gratitude is razor tight as her superior shakes his head and hands her a few notes of cash from his own immense wallet.

Get it sorted, he says.

Yes sir.

Today, Shoeberg.

Yes sir.

Boss: And find me this bloody kid! He could be anywhere—even in a ditch. Have you checked all the ditches? I don't want an answer to that. I have already ordered a full-scale search of all the ditches within a twenty five mile radius of the boy's home *and* his *school*. It's taken a lot of manpower. A lot of overtime. Very expensive, so whatever you're actually planning on doing next, you'll have to do it alone. I've spent all the money.

Yes sir.

There are no more resources.

Yes sir.

No, in fact, I just remembered, you will not be completely alone. In fact, I want you to work with Simms. Simms is very bright, and incredibly organised and has told me personally that he despises you. He will be your partner.

Yes sir.

Good. Now, there is one condition to Simms agreeing to work with you—and that's that you must not create any kind of stink or mess or bad atmosphere in his exquisite car.

You are drifting off a little now. Is any of this real?

Shoeberg nods, she raises her arms before getting herself to her feet, as though unable to fend off some physical, tendril-like presence of her superior officer's bullying jibes, or the unreasonableness of his requests, or his terrible policing.

Her mouth hangs open as she finally gets up to leave, pulling a big ugly shawl around herself. She grabs a shabby brown leather bag from somewhere near her feet and stuffs the cash directly inside it.

At her desk, in the busy police station, Shoeberg stares at the face of a young teenage boy who has obviously spent time as an army cadet. The missing boy. He is smiling and wearing a beret. His straw blond hair and flushed cheeks speak of a healthy enthusiasm for military-type activities. Shoeberg sniffs and wipes her nose. On her desk is a large sub-type sandwich. It's a made up brand, and you enjoy looking at the logo—which is two owl faces next to each other, drawn in gaudy red and brown lines.

The sandwich company is called SUB_OWL. The sandwich itself looks hugely inviting, a real achievement on the part of the edibles team in the props department. You actually want to eat the sandwich. You regret not cooking yourself any food, but just putting the grill on to high and then leaving it. You realise you haven't actually turned off the grill.

The grill is on in your kitchen.

But you want to see Shoeberg eat the sandwich. She reaches a hand out to it, she picks it up. She is so frail, you wonder if the sandwich will in fact eat her.

She opens her mouth. Her eyes roll back as she finally accepts the food into her mouth. But just as she is about to finally eat something, Simms arrives. She pauses with the SUB_OWL just millimetres from her mouth.

Boss! He says. Boss—no time for snacking, I'm afraid. Payroll want to see you.

Now? Says Shoeberg. The actor playing Shoeberg really nails a mournful note here. Her yearning for that sandwich is palpable. The actor has probably not eaten anything for weeks. She has been preparing to truly mourn for that sandwich. She probably had many painful conversations with the edible team in the props dept., telling the edible props assistant in detail how she was planning to starve herself, and swearing the assistant to secrecy while she took a near-suicidal plunge into starvation, just so this scene would work the way it does.

You can imagine the pained face of the edible props assistant, at home, not responding to his family who want to know how his big job in television is going. Ignoring his mother, who has put him up while he worked as an unpaid intern for three years. Forcing himself to avoid food in solidarity with the actor playing Shoeberg, whom he secretly loves, and yearns to call sister.

You zone back into what's happening on screen. Simms is belittling Shoeberg further with some news he has about the payroll dept.

Patrice is after you, and he looks furious. Apparently someone told our superior officer that you didn't get paid?

Who told him that?

How should I know? But you shouldn't annoy that lot in Payroll. Ruin your life, they can. If you get no-officed.

What's no-officed?

Ask Patrice, says Simms. He gestures in the direction of some other part of the office.

Shoeberg puts her sandwich down, rises ghoulishly from her seat, and leaves the shot, following the direction of Simms's outstretched hand into the distance. Simms, left alone with the massive, delicious-looking sandwich, picks it up. He sniffs it. He pulls an offended face. He chucks the sandwich in the bin.

There is a 15 second shot of the sandwich in the bin, nestled amongst balled up A4 paper and loads of pencil shavings. Glistening chipotle sauce oozes like lava, mingles with bits of dust and collects in the ridges of the bin. A skein of ham slowly unfurls.

Now they're in a corridor. Maybe outside payroll? Patrice the payroll clerk is giving Shoeberg another bollocking. How dare you? He's saying. We paid you in full, into the bank account you gave us. And you go into a senior leader's office and lie about me! You question my professionalism at the highest level, without even a phone call?

Shoeberg looks pitiful, coughing, her shoulders rising and falling, she is just bones. She says, But I didn't get any money. When I went to the bank, it took my card. I have nothing.

Well, you were probably so overdrawn that your entire salary didn't even get you back into the black.

I. I don't think so, that doesn't seem possible.

Patrice leans in very close to Shoeberg's face. You can tell he is probably a psychopath. You can imagine a future episode in which Patrice is revealed to have been the culprit in a spate of vicious attacks.

You are utterly pathetic, Patrice says. Everyone knows you can't even keep your head above water, despite being paid a good wage and having a tiny, cheap little flat. Everyone knows you're destitute because of your own shocking decision-making. And your tragic past is also a result of your feeble grasp of your life. I'm told you used to be a good detective, but there are plenty of people I would rather see in your job, all of them able to keep up with their DD payments. All of them capable of looking directly at their bank statement and seeing nothing to surprise them.

It's difficult, that's all. Listen, Patrice, please can you help me?

Yes, I can help you, says Patrice.

Oh thank God. Thank you, just a small advance is all . . .

Patrice stops her by raising a long, elegant hand. No, he says. I cannot help you like that. I can help you like this—look around you. Where are we?

In the corridor, says Shoeberg.

That's right, we're in the corridor. Not my office. Not your office. The corridor. This is an unofficial conversation. This is a chance for you to correct your mistake.

Oh.

Go and grovel to your superior officer. Make it clear you made a terrible mistake.

I can't—he's only interested in the case . . .

I don't think you have grasped the very precarious nature of the situation you're in, says Patrice. You are a corridor person now. Do you understand? Nobody will meet with you in an official place. Nobody will touch your files, your folders, overtime, equipment, expenses, your pension. You are a crack person. A gap. You are a person that doesn't technically even exist. Think about it. When was the last time anyone talked to you in their office?

Just now, I just came from

Not police! Not police people! Real people. When was the last time an administrator had a conversation with you that wasn't next to the vending machine, or in the carpark?

They just happened to catch me, that's all. It saves time . . .

Patrice raises his eyebrows. They are such meticulous eyebrows, they could in fact have been tailored for this exact expression. There is no word, you realise, for this experience. The experience of looking at someone's eyebrow and realising that you are under their power. This has happened to you in real life. You start thinking about this and then stop because of the action on the screen.

The actor playing Patrice is very gifted, but you realise that this role—immaculate administrative class with psychotic undertones—is probably a type he gets cast in, with very little variation between jobs.

After he stops looking this immaculate, there is nothing for this kind of actor. You don't know his name. You wonder if you read somewhere that his body had been found floating in the river, or if he had filmed himself masturbating in the bath and sent it to his young assistant.

Patrice stares at Shoeberg with redoubled contempt. No, he is saying, No, they do not happen to catch you. They come to you in the corridors because they cannot stand to have you in their space, in their proper, official space. You do not belong, Ms Shoeberg. Try it, if you don't believe me. Knock on this door. Go on.

He gestures to the door they happen to be standing next to. B12 is all it says on the door.

Knock on door B12, says Patrice. And see if the people inside are willing to admit you.

B12?

Yes, B12. Do you even know what they do in there?

I . . .

The whole time Patrice is talking, Shoeberg has been fazing out. She looks pale. Her lips are blue. With great effort, she turns away from Patrice and staggers off, leaning on the walls as she goes, dragging herself across numerous informative posters (that have been designed from scratch by the excellent professionals in the props team).

Suddenly you remember you have left the grill on! You leap up and run into the kitchen, your heart is pounding. This is worse than the beetle! When you get there, you realise that you have left the grill on, but you actually didn't put any food on the grill.

You find a collection of the food things you have recently bought form the corner shop. You stand at the worktop and shove ham then white bread then ham then butter into your mouth. You chew and swallow just enough to allow room for more stuff. You ram in some monster munch crisps. You are panting with the ferocity of your own eating. You can hear shouting on the TV. Or sex. It could be either.

When you come back, for some reason, Shoeberg is at home.

Simms is drying himself with a ragged towel after taking a shower in Shoeberg's flat. He stalks into her bedroom, all skin and muscle and silhouettes of pubes. He tosses the towel onto the floor and languidly starts to get dressed.

Nobody can know about this, he says, pulling on a long, argyle-patterned sock.

Shoeberg nods absently. She's lying on her bare mattress, partly covered by a thin sheet. She blows a scrap of hair away from her face.

I need some money, Simms says.

What for?

To get my clothes washed, Simms says. I stink of sex.

Can't you just do that at home, she whispers.

Think about it for a second, Simms says. Just think about what you just said. Joan will notice, yeah? I need to get it done express. It's a lot of fucking around.

There is a silence while Shoeberg wrestles with the idea of giving this man her money.

It's in my bag, she says.

Ta.

He pulls all of Shoeberg's recently acquired money out of her brown satchel and puts it into his pocket. It is many, many times the amount required to wash Simms's clothes. She nods again, watching it go. Then, as Simms starts to leave, she sits up.

Wait! Where are you going? We still have to look for the missing Cadet.

Simms grimaces. He's gone, Shoeberg. Why do you think we ended up doing that again?

I don't know.

Because he's dead.

He's not dead.

That cadet is dead and you needed to be consoled.

Shoeberg looks as though the effort of speaking is becoming too much. Her voice rattles as she adds, Please! And reaches out a hand towards Simms.

Simms does not disguise his revulsion, now that he is clean, he wants to get out. Can't. Sorry. I have to go to the cake shop—wife's birthday. Special evening etc.

There is a long silence. Simms looks at Shoeberg on the bed. He finally seems to show a shred of human decency.

Look, Shoeberg. Thank you for saving my life today. I'm sorry this er—whatever this is. I'm sorry because I know it's shit what I'm doing. I'm running away. I'm taking your money. I gave you pity sex. But I have to go. You can hate me if you want.

Shoeberg shrugs. She looks down at herself, under her little sheet.

Just go, she says.

Thanks. I'll save you some cake

Actually, could you leave some of that money? It's been a while since I ate . . .

Simms is doing up his tie. Of course! He says. I'm not a total asshole. He winks without smiling. He leaves the door open as he goes out, without leaving any money behind.

Shoeberg lies alone in her bed for five minutes. The camera angles change so we can see every detail of her poverty as she goes over whatever happened with Simms in the bed, and presumably, whatever happened while you were eating crisps. Will she give you any clues about what led to her saving Simms's life? Is she any closer to saving the life of the missing cadet?

The camera agonises over her. An obsessive for her fingernails, her palms, her wrists, her wrinkled elbows, her one visible shoulder blade, her collarbone, her jaw. You wonder, will she stop breathing? Did the actor playing her collapse during the filming of this scene? She is so still, she could be dead. How long is left of the episode?

Then, with a gasp, she forces herself up, she struggles across the bed in her sagging underwear. Now she's making coffee in the kitchenette, letting in a little streetlight come in through the window and fuzz up in the kettle steam. She nips at sugar from a spoon before putting it into the cup and stirring. She takes the coffee back to her bedroom.

Something has occurred to her, but there is no indication what it could be. Everything has happened while you were in the kitchen with your food and your failure to turn off the grill.

In fact, you should pay attention because the grill is still on and you are shrinking faster now than before. Soon you may not even be able to reach the controls for the grill.

Shoeberg is back on the bed, sitting cross-legged, she digs a file out of her massive brown satchel-type bag thing. You marvel again at the quality of the props department in this programme.

She lays out pictures of places and people you do not recognise, except one of them, you think, may have been an actor in the Harry Potter films. She analyses the pictures. She looks at them. Then she turns, leans away and stretches down the side of the bed. She returns with a scabby-looking laptop. She cannot connect to the internet.

Shit, she says. She pulls on a dressing gown.

She's outside the front door of a flat in her dressing gown. The door opens, a student stands in the doorway, she has hair in her face and a surly, educated arrogance in her smile. She resembles a costume based on Shoeberg's dismal circumstances.

But peeping from beneath a pastel blue M&S dressing gown is a classic X-Ray Specs t-shirt. The student's obvious hidden financial power makes Shoeberg hesitate.

Hi, I live upstairs. For some reason my internet isn't working. Can I er, I don't know the word, borrow your Wi-Fi?

The student shakes her head and sighs. Jesus, again? You still owe us from last time.

Sorry.

Fine. It's fifty quid though.

I'll give it to you next week—they're late paying me at work.

The student again shakes her head. She says Jesus. She looks at Shoeberg like she is a piece of shit.

You want the password?

Yes please.

OK, it's Pathetic Upstairs Loser ACAB

All one word?

All one word.

Any caps?

Capital P on pathetic, U on Upstairs and L on Loser. ACAB is always all caps.

Thanks.

The student shuts the door in Shoeberg's face.

Shoeberg is back in her bedroom. She sits on her bed. She is looking at something on the screen. Her face is somehow full of hope, yet racked with the inevitable failure of whatever she's trying to do.

We see her typing the words Sycamore Plough into BLANDIT, a made up search engine (this invented brand is nowhere near as subversive or clever as the SUB_OWL sandwich wrapping you saw earlier, but it's still pretty good. It's called BLANDIT DELIVERS and it has a picture of a kind of highwayman as its avatar. This is presumably a reference to the Information Super Highway. But you wonder if anyone else is going to get that reference. Also, it makes you think that this time the art department people have gone too far. Like, they have redefined what a search engine fundamentally is, just for the sake of this one scene—also you are shrinking you are absolutely shrinking to nothing. What will you do? If you could only get down from the sofa, but that feels impossibly far now. You consider trying to hypnotise a rat, would that work? You try to tell your family, or anyone, that you have downsized too far and things are really bad now and could someone come and help) Shoeberg clicks 'Deliver' and then the screen fills with results.

She clicks the top one and the shadowy faces of a group of men appear, they are walking through a dark carpark—they seem to have been captured on CCTV outside a factory called Sycamore Plough. Music plays, insisting that this blurry image of shadowy men has some meaning to the programme, but you missed the relevance because you were in the kitchen stuffing crisps and milk into your mouth.

The lights go out in Shoeberg's room.

No, moans Shoeberg. Not now. Not this now.

But it's too late, the promise of those unpaid bills you saw earlier has been delivered upon. She's been cut off. She goes from room to pitch black room, using the faces of the gang on her laptop screen as a kind of torch. Her flat in this light is a monstrous landscape. Her silhouette in the lounge is abject. She stands there, finally defeated by how shit everything is.

And then, rising up behind her in the gloom seems to be the hairy, grotesque shape of a monster/

BLEEEP BLEEEEP BLEEEEP YOU REALLY SHOULD HAVE TURNED OFF THE GRILL BLEEEEP BLEEEEP BLEEEP

CARL LANDAUER

Innocent Man on the Run

Alfred Hitchcock's *The 39 Steps* after
Richard Buchan's *The Thirty-Nine Steps*

Gone is Buchan's "man on the spot,"
the colonial made sick by
        the talk of the ordinary Englishman,
the man whose life on the veld
gave him bird-of-prey vision,
who knew when
        you are hemmed in on all sides,
the key to escape is to stay in place
        and let your enemies find you,
but now cornered
        in a table-cloth of a place.
A Rhodesian who finds horror in this
        cold-blooded indoor business,
not like the violent deaths abroad.
In the London flat he needed brandy
despite deaths he inflicted in the Matabele War.
The knifed American on his floor
was no warrior slaughtered
in one of Victoria's small wars
waged against other races
at the edge
of the crimson map.

Instead, we get Hitchcock's nattily dressed
   Canadian,
the Canadian who through days of running
never needs a shave.
We get camera angles and framing
learned in Berlin,
the sculptural phone with its shading,
ringing ominously in the frame,
and the char woman's silent, open mouth,
cutting quickly at finding the dead American
to the shrieking train whistling
and steam rushing out of the tunnel,
carrying our Canadian
to an obscure Scottish point.

All eyes on Mr. Memory,
the little mustachioed man
regurgitating millions
of facts and figures,
who can tell you every fighter's name and
   weight
and the round when he won a belt
in St. Louis or New York,
as well as the military secrets
at the center of Hitchcock's tale,
with carnival music,
a haunting signal of menace
as the black-and-white action
begins and ends.

EXACTING CLAM

ERIC T. RACHER

Two Poems

On the IDEOLOGY OF America [SIC] as semeiotic, or, On the BIRTH OF a nation

Odysseus discovered America in the early-to-mid 1860s, as the Calypso of Elvis's
hips rose from a river of begats into the pure *potentia* of Cotton Mather's damp
and dangling remnants' vast unravelling—*if there is to be a nation one must begin
somewhere*, if not one risks *slipping, slipping, slipping into nothing at all.*

Odysseus and his men proceeded to slay the native inhabitants, flay their bodies,
make sandals of their skins, which they decorated with precious stones & gold.
They then stooped down & bound them on to walk forward thro' Eternity,
across the wilderness, from sea to shining sea. But they say that *if there is to be*

a sestet one must begin somewhere and in this sestet they say that every day
a *pure product of America* signs up for an Expense of Spirit® customer loyalty card
for cash back on every purchase of premium blend certified-organic Selfhood.

They say that History demands human sacrifice, feeds on human hearts. O William Carlos
   Williams, they say,
wherefore art thou William Carlos Williams? Deny thy father
and refuse thy name. 'Tis but thy name that is my enemy. O be some other name.

WITH a sestet mostly stolen FROM one OF RobeRT FRost's letters, or, on MacheRey's statement that Defoe 'made the island the indispensable setting, the scene FOR an ideological motif which was only beginning to emerge: the meditation on origins' as contrasted with Donne's claim that 'no sonnet is an island, entire of itself; every sonnet is a piece of the continent, a part of the main'

"In every American [Sonnet –*ed.*]
there is an air of incorrigible innocence,
which seems to conceal a diabolical
cunning," A.E. Housman said to Frederick
Prokosch (Or was it to Billy Collins?),
whom he also asked "Is your air of simplicity
a part of your cunning, or is your cunning
just an aspect of your inner simplicity?"
But perhaps it is the country's fault. [You may
be right, Herr Frost; *cf.* here Melville, 1857.]
*A young country is too easily satisfied
with a mechanical proficiency in the arts
that can at best never be better than amateurish.
The country may not expect enough.*

Jennifer M. Phillips

Two Poems

Starry, Starry Night

Remember that December drive, when night
scraped the pigment from the canvas and the stars shone through?
A keen virginal wind tried all the chinks and crevices with its pliant plaint around the
cabin we had rented by the lake, and light lapped at our edges.

Too much time we were roiled and tumbled by the breaking
ubiquitous surf of loss and death's gasp and grasp
and the young ones going down like sunk ships around us; all the
stammering silences spreading after last exhalations

like skins of ice closing over a pond. Your fingers
struck tender sparks on my skin's tinder. Maybe it was just kindness, that
borealis arcing, but joy enough to go on embering
in memory through galey decades after, a glow of gladness hung across my sky.

It was your place of childhood, layered like a blanket-chest
with your warmest, best times. I came, as to a shrine in a ruined forest,
with reverence for what did not remain for me to see, but was palpable, nevertheless.
For you perhaps a reworking of your old elements. We went walking

under the musty-sweet hemlocks, inhaled dusty white-pine perfume,
needle-mast all give beneath our feet. We propped our lager cans on the green sill
blistered by many distant summer suns as the latest one went down
with its slow inevitability and the snow at last came.

Sprung

Sky the color of old dust under the bed. Rain on the way. How
is it we find ourselves waiting it out again—waiting any of it out
in our scarcity?
Hummingbirds fritter round the unblooming maples. Still as
cold as March two months later, but

the push is on.

Magnolia buds ajar.
Flocks crossing in the night like Passover angels. Morning
opens its other pharaonic eye.

Raspberry canes vault
upward and spider across the ditches. Doves in the grass are bent on
wooing and pursuit.

Can't be coy. It's on the wing.
One reservoir fills to straining,

overtops its levees,
while we are leaning on our shovels. Another
dwindles and dries.

Children run through the sprinklers, leave
all the taps running and the lights on.

Time, that rattlesnake
we have no idea of lying in wait. Time, whittling away at us all the while. Fiddle tune
repeating endlessly in our palaces.

Smell of smoke.

Stephen Bett

Umberto Eco, *The Name of the Rose*

(section heading; trans. William Weaver)

In which Adso writhes in the torments of love, then William arrives with Venantius's text, which remains undecipherable even after it has been deciphered.

We forgot to say please
an ass-backward *sign*, surely

AS if,   from Asbo to Adso [1]
it doesn't add up
(clunk to monk)

Signif·i·cant grapheme drag
—pls decipher

*(In which Adso, in the scriptorium, reflects on the
history of his order and on the destiny of books)*

The dumb luck of cooked books

The disorderliness of their
Novel Lines [2]

[1] See *Novel Lines 101*, "Martin Amis, *Lionel Asbo*"
[2] The italicized lines: another section heading in *The Name of the Rose*

Nat Raum

i explain animal crossing to my lover

a dog runs the town hall and a raccoon
owns the general store. hedgehog sisters

dictate fashion trends; a pigeon pours you
your daily café au lait. a blue squirrel
tells you his furniture is just like him,
only softer, and you understand

completely. a macaroni penguin sends
you a gift in the mail and you nearly cry,

overcome by the kindness you find
so rare in your day to day. your neighbors
all ask if you are okay when you spend
too long playing. your baseline was never

okay. you barely remember the game
without strife to surround you. in fact,

the island may be a metaphor for your fervent
desire to hear a little more waves crashing
on perfect powder-sands, a little less grief
in your heart. you have learned

to shift shapes in ways that would break
other people's bones; to say you start

up system, travel via biplane to remote
oceanside getaway, and pass several hours
in a state you could only describe
as sedated—to say you do it all

as a way to unwind would still be,
to you, putting it lightly.

Tom Formaro

Two Poems from Advice for My Daughter

Morning Constitutional

I asked God the odds of survival
    They said keep moving in zeroes

but not close to home—Look carefully in
    the flowering vines for a more perfect union

and station the latent miscalculations
    at the center of the labyrinth one brick

at a time   and again after the reign
    Please exchange your clockworks for

unbooked questions about where time
    ended and what's needed to heed the mind

My friend Emily says her prayers walking
    backwards because they make more sense

now that she's been reported to authorities
    for believing in hypotheticals and text symbols

Starting With a Line from Patrizia Cavalli

It must have been spring. In fact was.
A hyphenated spring—imperfected in its
way. Or its preference. Just to say—
via a worn night left out in the cold—
plums wrapped in parchment can hold
periodic days with lines just so. And
what wintered air remains unclaimed
in the cellar reeking of rhubarb wine?
It took years to clear my mother's house
of facts and fermented ephemera. Yet
spring might have been and fact might
have was—but only on the night north
of the Quonset hut destroyed by the
derecho too early in spring to have been

Emily Adams

Two Poems

Such Short Mercies

Thank you, but I know what the dreams mean.
I know by now this is but one iteration—
stars, coneflowers, etc. The point beyond the reach
of language, which shifts and shifts again.
What percentage of a life is meant to be
remembering? Forget it. Let some God finally come
and confirm me in the church of relative happiness.
I shiver in my bed, and all night I pick myself clean.

Unimaginable

For three whole years I did nothing
without getting high first.
Call it whatever you want,
it was also survival. We were all
trying to weather what felt
to everyone like an onslaught,
an endless stream of vicious storms.
But most alarming: I couldn't
keep our plants from dying—
brown from the bottom
every damn time, no matter
how much sun, rain, tending.

You were right all along.
Being tender solved nothing—
that itself being its own
unimaginable loss.

Eric Weiskott

Four Poems

Preferences

Her desire to be tied up versus his to be served.

Compromise is possible,
but sexual congress is our loneliest form of government.

Her desire to be incarcerated versus his to be elect.

A stadium is ancient architecture
for containing and apportioning fantasy.

I love you because with you I feel least alone.

Through language I conceal that part of myself I'd prefer
to share with you. *Are you at daycare yet,*

did you arrive, please pass my wallet.

Anne Carson writes that sex is like money or language,
a substitute.

Come to find, life is mostly substitution.

The language of money pinches like desire.
Through it we consent

to our form of government,

which is the language of consent.
This too is a transposition.

I consent to our children,

to our bread, to our argument,
I consent to the senate of crows erect and alert

on yon telephone wire. These days,

I love you because I feel alone.
The poem: ancient architecture.

Come to find, I conceal that part of myself.

Barcarolle

BARCAROLLE: An Italian river song in triple measure.

Visual memory is poor (compared to auditory).
It is easier to hear with the mind's eye
       than to see with ears of another world:

listen to this barcarolle
the torch being carried across
       the threshold of another world.

It is easier to relinquish
the sensation of rocking,
       the sensation of sight,

than a barcarolle when in Venice.
I can't remember your face just now.
       The torch of sight

departs before blind darkness arrives
in Venice or anywhere,
       the threshold of another song.

I see in my mind's eye
a boat,
       another world.

Meditation

In my crawlspace fiddling
 with some plastic snaptop bins
             I'm thinking about lunch plans
  and John Wayne Gacy
and final wishes.
  The arch of a sepulcher
             through which a form of prayer escapes.
 The bins contain Christmas ornaments
although I am Jewish
 (although I am no longer a Jew)
             because my atheist wife believes in the form
 of Christmas. Gacy drew
diagrams for the boys
 he hired to dig man-sized holes
             who did not know they were digging graves.
 The leakage of his 33 murders
found its exacting formal container
 in gravely annotated diagrams
             of a crawlspace. To dig a hole
 without knowing what it is for
only certain that it is deepening
 like a sepulchral chord.
             I'm finished fiddling:
 I back out doubled over
so I appear to be bowing.

Bob Dylan's Voice[1]

contains its own photonegative
a blue note upon the deep.
Voice is beyond communication
a collect call from fortune
a new word for desperation
wailing of chimes
way out among the mountain laurel.

The endless road runs straight
into the garden gates
and on through the Temple of Dagon.
I couldn't help but follow
a stuttering foot inside the meter
a palace of mirrors
architecture of the larynx.

No angel's voice whispers
across a changed Mississippi.
until cruel death.
Forty-eight Minnesotas later
the dark room of his mind
stitches still mending
rough melisma.

[1] Bob Dylan, "Changing of the Guards," *Street-Legal* (1978), and "High Water (For Charley Patton)," *"Love and Theft"* (2001).

Brooke Mitchell

Two Poems

Who Are You and Who Do You Love? After Bhanu Kapil

The moon's bitter daughter; waxing tongues. Modifier, or always in relation to; independents. A stiff blanket; cold winter woman with nothing warmer to fall into. Aster cropped up on a cliffside in Maine, first flower in America with dewy leaves at dawn; the sun creeping over the Atlantic. My mothers best intentions; my father over the phone from his rehab, reminding him there will be no car to drive him home if he signs out early. A red cedar chest; a grandmother's crocheted blankets piled inside. Iron kettle; tea. Sharp wind aching a cheek; eyes tightened, mouth pinched in response. My father's best intentions; me, three weeks after he comes home, when I hug him again for the first time.

From Image

Shadows softening the dip between jaw and cheekbone

Ceramic scrape against wooden countertop

Human photographs human through Skype

Cubed beef coats slime over palm, under fingernails

Eyebrows edged into place

Ring light buzzing; a girlfriend's chatter

Camera captures camera output

Captures germs glazed brown in the open, uncooked

Nose playing pale clay, peaked and light-dipped

Cork squeaking from merlot bottle

We learn to love through image

Meat is for eating, not art

Scalp layered with a hush of hair, whispering crowd.

Gluggled pours into crystal glasses

We learn image from a distance

To butcher is to mourn, thank, not play

There are lips, collarbones, freckles clotting their chest

Red plastic filter slipping across camera lens

P.J. Blumenthal

Five Poems

From a Far Country

When young he moved to a far country.
A river led to it and a mountain and a valley
and then another river
sinuous like a question mark.
There he lay with a girl,
 pale as snow.
She knotted her legs around him,
"Never let me go" she said.
When he was older he opened a shop,
sold groceries to traders.
Then came the famine and the threats of war.
It was an age without telephones,
and letters from home were rare.
In dreams he saw them all.
Some faces he knew.
Others he did not recall despite the familiarity.
For his neighbors he was the stranger,
and yet, in hard times
they did not treat him like one.
When the war was over he was old.
Once more he traveled down the river
sinuous like a question mark
across the valley over the mountain
and down the river that led to home.
Everything was as it had always been.
The faces he had seen in his dreams,
those he recognized and those he did not,
had not changed, nor the places.
"Why is it that I am old
and you are all the same?" he asked.
But no one could say.
Instead they celebrated his return,
showed him to his house
and clothed him in the local way.
When he looked into the mirror
he saw that he was young.
He wanted to tell of the far country,
of the toils, the wars,
but he lacked the words and the opportunity,
and the celebrations lingered long into the day
till the sun hung low in the west a pink light
and the mountains glowed purple
and the first stars pierced through the night
like eyes or full-stops
at the end of a sentence.

Ode to my Inferiority Complex

I owe a lot to you:
this house we share,
the vintage furniture,
the view from the window
where we watch the others,
the happy ones, go by,
even the way I talk.
Once when I was young
I whispered my dreams to you.
"No," you said, "you aren't old enough,"
"They will not take you seriously."
Later when I'd learned to hesitate
you were always understanding.
"No rush, there is time."
 Those were your words not mine.
Then I was old, and one day
you said:
"Why have you waited so long?
Soon you'll be dead."
These days you're an expert in silence.
Maybe you're just tired,
not that I mind.
Anyway, I don't need your advice anymore.
Remember how we used to sit in the café,
hand in hand envying the beautiful?
They always have more fun than us.
That's what we'd think, the two of us
though too ashamed to say it,
even to each other.
I wish I knew whose idea
it was back then, yours or mine,
to buy this house so far from town.
It doesn't really matter now,
and you won't tell me anyhow.
Hey, don't think I haven't noticed
that you're angry with me again.

In a Toilet at the Amerikahaus

The utmost station of an exile.
This last piece of home.
I don't know what crime I committed anymore.
The memory of shuffling-footed policemen
beating at the door
may just be fantasy now.

Here I am at this outpost.
My culture reduced to a small thing: a house.
Not even the librarians speak my language;
the pictures on the wall vague images
   of places I may have known.
Is the librarian throwing glances at me?
Or am I thinking romantically?
The woman at the coat-check counter
is glaring through her glasses,
her hands knitting socks for pink grandchildren
or nooses for strangers.

What I hate most is a house
where you hear your own footsteps.

Once I had a love
with hair so fine
she twined
it above me
to keep me warm.
"I know the wind is cold," she'd say,
"and I pity those out there in the dark
whose tracks none will find in the falling leaves."
I recall that love as heat and moisture now,
at a loss for other names.

I am thinking this in a toilet
                    in the Amerikahaus
while planning my final response.
The tiled walls, the tiled floors, the porcelain
awaken only loneliness and desire
in all
who scribble their desperate graffiti
                    in these stalls,
warmth's aftermath recalled.

Some take recourse in self-love
or in notes,
long and mostly unrhymed
 like this one,
printed on a page
white as a wall.

Why I killed Pasolini

We were like two nations
at war:
he some mysterious Greek,
I his Turkey.
He had written about me
for years
manufactured images
of my coast lines
the curves of my hills
and the inhabitants of my
murmuring foreign cities.
Sometimes he had even been among us
but never of us
distant rather
like a camera's eye.
To be his point of focus
turned me to object.
To his images
I answered with my own:
Yes
let these international boundaries
spill over into dream fear,
let the flesh projection charge
where the light projection ends.
Time to pull a switch, baby.
This time it's me you see,
the images removed,
tossed on the junk heap
in the forechambers of the real temple.
It is no light task to penetrate these mysteries.
To see the next image
demands the murder
of all half truths.

I'm Horny

I'm
tired of reading comic books
with suggestive images
and fuck films haven't done the trick.
My eyes jerk urgently from body to body
yearning to call a thousand faces
indiscriminately you.
The streets are no solace now
nor is solitude
and the violent grip between my legs
in what I think of as passionate privacy
lacks the warmth of your caress.
Maybe I should study politics
or economics
or open a shop somewhere,
sell nuts and dried goods,
or maybe find a job
at the university
teaching Shakespeare or Catullus
or Emily Dickinson.
The thought of you
is a problem for me.
You multiply like a house of mirrors
leaving me spinning in your reflections.
I want you
and I don't want you.
Better a dog who will lick me afterwards
then forget.
You do not come alone
nor do I.
We never do.
We bring our representatives
and while we as they say
make love
our envoys are plotting new wars
some immediate
some yet to come.
Either way we lose
whether we meet or not
and the whole history of Europe
is hung up on our horniness.

Jean Lorrain

Jean Lorrain (1855–1906) was the pseudonym of Paul Alexandre Martin Duval. He was born on 9 August 1855 in Fécamp, Seine-Maritime, France and by the time he was twenty-five, he was one of the leading figures of the Decadent Movement and the author of numerous novels, volumes of poetry and short stories. He was also associated with the Symbolist school and can be seen as a key literary figure who successfully made the transition from Symbolist to Decadent. Lorrain was a dedicated disciple of dandyism and spent much of his time amongst the fashionable artistic circles in France, particularly in the cafés and bars of Montmartre.

In 1897, he was challenged to a duel by Marcel Proust because Lorrain had publicly questioned the nature of Proust's relationship with Lucien Daudet, implying they were lovers. Proust challenged Lorrain to a pistol duel to defend his honour and his reputation against the accusations. Both men survived the duel.

Lorrain was openly homosexual, often citing ancient Greece as the noble heritage for his homosexuality. He became colloquially known as 'The Ambassador of Sodom'. He began to use morphine as a way of combatting symptoms of tuberculosis. When that failed, he moved on to ether, a habit he shared with Guy de Maupassant. Lorrain wrote a handful of horror stories under the influence of ether, but he eventually abandoned its use when the substance gave him stomach ulcers and associated health problems.

By the 1920s, despite being the author of fourteen novels, five poetry collections, twenty novellas, fifty-eight short stories, ten plays, three travel books, and a libretto, as well as hundreds of pieces of journalism that he had contributed to the satirical weekly *Le Courrier français*, Jean Lorrain had been virtually forgotten by the literary world, his works overshadowed by the achievements of Baudelaire, Poe, Stenbock, Wilde, Huysmans, and Rachilde.

Lorrain is one of those literary figures whose life and art were bound together into the an almost seamless whole. He embodied, more inescapably than anyone else, the absurdities, the affectations, the paradoxes and the perversities of the Decadent lifestyle and the Decadent worldview.

His most successful Decadent novels were *Monsieur de Bougrelon* (1897), and *Monsieur de Phocas* (1901); *Sensations et souvenirs,* published in 1895, was his most successful short story collection.

Although his novels and stories are written in another time, as well as in another language, Lorrain's detailed descriptions of fin-de siècle France, the feverish, nightmarish atmosphere of his wonderfully decadent and sophisticated tales, mean that he can be considered to be one of the true chroniclers of the fin-de-siècle. His subtle social commentary is evident in stories in which he effortlessly conveys the particular sensibility of La Belle Epoque.

Jean Lorrain

The Man Who Made Wax Heads

Translated by RJ Dent

To Henry Bauër

She followed me like an obsession. Hers was a woman's face which, it's true, gave an impression of muteness. She had a straight nose, hard blue eyes, and beneath her blond hair which was pulled back in two small pigtails that started near her temples, she had a rather prominent forehead that was lined with obstinacy. Her hair, bright, soft and yellow crowned her like a helmet, and fell to the nape of her neck so that it looked like a metal collar. But on that stubbornly mute face, the greatest attraction was, like a true mystery, the smile; a scarlet smile with full and sinuous lips, as if sealed by some unbreakable promise the imperious smile of a soul that denies itself, a smile that did not smile.

Modelled in wax, the head was intricately delicate in tone and detail, and in the dim light of the studio, which I had just followed Gormas into, that head, motionless on its base, almost supernatural in the intensity of its proud mouth and lapis eyes, said no. Was it the twilight? In the ambiguous surroundings of the studio that was cluttered with all manner of objects, old clothes, and the white nakedness of statues vaguely animated by the night, an imperceptible frown, doubtless due to some play of light, seemed to accentuate its indomitable expression of defiance.

"*Symphonica eroïca;* the heroic symphony," Gormas whispered in my ear as I approached the base, trying to decipher the strange words that were written on it.

"Yes, it is, quite simply, equal to Beethoven's heroic symphony, but the curious thing is that the woman depicted on that head with its unwilling smile, its predatory profile, actually exists. From morning to evening, she walks through the streets of Auteuil and you can meet her there every day."

"A model?" I ventured, intrigued.

"No, not at all. She agreed to climb onto the model table for one time only, and persuading her wasn't without difficulty. She didn't want to become a goddess, but I begged her until she agreed. And you have to admit, it would have been a great shame if such a woman hadn't agreed to let such a vision be evoked."

With his hands behind his back, Gormas, like me, stared in admiration at the painted wax eyes that appeared to have become dreamily distant.

"Yes, she reconciles one with life," he said, continuing his train of thought, "and she almost consoles one for the boredom of walking there. One can see such creatures there, and even then does one really see them? No, because if you passed Rayon-d'Aube (that's what I call her) in the street, you wouldn't recognize her. The best proof is that you've already seen her a hundred times and she hasn't made the slightest impression on you. A pretty woman passing by is either a possible or sometimes an impossible night, if one is prepared to spend five or twenty louis,

give or take. After all, what one desires at twenty is different to what one desires at our age. Sadly, one looks at a young woman with a sigh of regret and lets her go elsewhere. One grows so weary, so far removed from others and from oneself that one's heart becomes afraid. What's the point of trying again? There is nothing true about women except for the idea we have of them. We sing romantic songs to dolls and as soon as the singer has something in his belly, the doll becomes a statue. Look at this wax head, Rayon-d'Aube is a beautiful, pale, blonde woman that Paris has kept hidden. Ringel met her and drew from her this mysterious face of heroism and refusal."

"So it's Ringel we have to thank," I said. And then I asked: "Who is Ringel?"

"Ringel," Gormas replied, "is a very curious, little-known artist that I think will interest you. I'll introduce you... He lives just a stone's throw from here, on Avenue du Point-du-Jour. Meet me here tomorrow morning and I'll take you to his studio, but let me give him notice. He's very touchy, very eccentric, and a bit wild. He confines himself to the gatehouse of the Champ de Mars, as well as the Champs-Élysées, for after having been presented with the Medal of Honour there, he believes himself to be persecuted, the victim of a cabal or at least of an injustice, and doesn't willingly let anyone enter his studio unless they're invited. He's quite violent, has the temperament of an adventurer, and the physique of a Renaissance military leader, he will no doubt be of great interest to you. But it is getting dark, so let me light a few lamps."

"There's no need," I told him. "I have to be going."

And having announced my departure, I left.

W e went through a wrought iron gate into a small courtyard. On the other side of the courtyard was a shed with a glass roof. There was a ring attached to a rope that when pulled set a rusty bell ringing. After a while, a tall, slim, muscular man in a tight-fitting blue sweater half-opened the shed door.

"Come in!" he shouted.

It was Ringel.

I sat in his studio, which was cluttered with monumental chalky white statues, and placed on shelves here and there were the disturbing and frozen smiles of painted wax heads, and I watched that graceful, tall, blonde man with a tanned complexion, as if he had been browned and then reheated, as he bustled around a large piece of wet clay that he was sketching, with the agility of a clown and the attentive suppleness of a watchful cat, I couldn't help but go through my memory for all of the absurd and crazy stories that I had been told about this Ringel.

His expressive and tenacious head, his sardonic, sensual mouth and even the colour of his warm complexion that was darker than the pale blond of his moustache, were certainly the features of a man of adventure and audacity, and he looked like one of those brave half Lorraine, half German companions that the Duke of Guise had brought to the Court of the Valois and which one is always surprised to find, in the chronicles of the era, nonchalantly leaning, a dagger in one hand, a cup and ball in the other, under the fleur-de-lis coffered ceilings of the Louvre, with a smile sharpened by the corruption of the times, one of those dangerous and sophisticated men who became Italians during the Florentine intrigues of Henri III and Catherine.

Almost opposite me was a plaster cast of a large naked woman with an ambiguous smile. She was leaning, or rather half-leaning, towards a small mirror she held in her hand. Her wavy hair, decorated with threads of pearls, was certainly that of a Madame de Sauve or one of those perverted and perverting maids of honour employed by Madame Catherine to dissipate the energy and lessen the determination of the partisans of the Béarnais or the Lorrain, the enemies of the king. If the theory of avatars is true, it was in some corridor hung with tapestries in the castles of Blois or Amboise that Ringel must have once encountered this insidious and smiling creature. She smelled of traps, ambush and lust, and on the night of Saint Bartholomew's Day she must certainly have, like many women of that time, passionately embraced the murderer of the day in the bed still warm from the previous day's activities, very happy to find the taste of the blood of the murdered on the lips of the chosen lover of the moment.

Perversity was the statue's title, and I remembered the scandal it had caused in 1878 at the Salon, and the uproar and outrage that had been stirred up by the warm transparency of its flesh, the polish of its thighs and the pink moisture of its lips; for the figure was entirely made of wax, and it palpitated in its equivocal and delightful pose with such life that it was able to emanate danger and exasperate desire. The public reacted to it as if it had committed an act of indecency, so much so that certain people in high places became very upset, and orders were given to remove the scandalous statue.

Obviously the artist objected to this. On having his objection dismissed by the court, he refused to recognise the judiciary's right to suppress his work and, with the violent determination of a man from another era, he had stood guard for two nights, revolver in hand, in front of his wax figure. And just like a heroic knight who would stand guard outside his lady's chambers, ready to resort to any means to protect her, when the commissioners that had been sent by the authorities came to remove the statue, the sculptor bravely engaged in the struggle at the feet of his *Perversity*, which, after being rocked and pulled from all sides, broke into pieces and collapsed onto its base, a strange symbol of a work not wanting to survive the affront inflicted on its creator.

That Benvenuto Cellini-style adventurer was indeed very much like the man himself, and the more I looked at him with his bold profile, his closely shaved head, and his muscular shoulders beneath the heavy cut of his fleece, the more easily I pictured him standing proudly in front of his statue, arms crossed over his chest, standing up to the crowd and challenging anyone to touch his work. And why had his *Perversity* suddenly collapsed? Was it pure chance; was there not something of the sorcerer about the man?

He had returned from Florence or at least from the court of Valois where in between his time with Madame Catherine and René the Florentine, he had lived in a society that was entirely devoted to the science of potions and bewitchments. Consequently, he must have brought back some mysterious secrets of the occult and the alchemist's art; for amongst the plaster busts and clay masks there were, peculiarly, the two wax heads upon which my gaze now lingered: two heads modelled in the Florentine style with thick hair that haloed the forehead like a nimbus, both clearly figures of the Renaissance.

One of the heads was of a boy aged somewhere between twenty and twenty-five years, with a sharp profile, thick, beardless lips, a jutting jaw, and with the thumbprint of the sculptor on his chin. It vaguely recalled the portraits of Lorenzo de Medici that were on display in galleries and museums. The cavalry officer's gorge, the curve of the cuirass, and the steel plates of the helmet covering brown curly hair completed the arrangement; it was a vigorous and bold work.

The other, on the contrary, was the head of a woman or a young, effeminate boy with pale, pink lips which pouted stubbornly. The pale translucence of his slightly feverish flesh and the look of terror of his eyes was evidence that he had lived and experienced intense suffering, and I do not know what cruel memories emanated from that terrified and mute young head.

> The painful, ardent and sickly head
> Has in the sombre charms of its native grace
> The attractions of a virgin and a perverse boy.
>
> Favourite of a bishop or learned Ophelia,
> His enigma is suffering, intoxication, madness
> Which like a black potion flows into his green eyes.

Certainly, those bruised eyes and that pallor spoke volumes in their silence; she had suffered in her flesh and in her soul. Into what horrible pleasures had she been initiated? But, as I looked into that child's eyes, eyes which had become the eyes of a woman by dint of staring at some atrocious nightmare, an inexplicable sense of pity seized me, heightened by unhealthy curiosity.

It was in the castle of Tiffauges, the lair of Gilles de Rais, that I first encountered the sinister truth regarding that terror-stricken head, and then, inevitably, several mysterious stories came back to me about the candle makers of the Middle Ages and the public disapproval attached to certain aspects of their trade. I heard that they lived in cellars, in an eternal chiaroscuro conducive to magic and apparitions Their visionary art (with which they invoked the real image of life) was closely related to that of sorcery: rituals and rites were carried out using wax figures. Witchcraft trials are full of references to them being used, and there was one legend that haunted me above all, that of the Anspach sculptor who slowly extracted the soul and life from his model to animate his painted wax and, once his masterpiece was completed, waited for nightfall to go and bury the corpse in one of the ditches of the earthworks.

Had Ringel guessed my thoughts?

"That pretty head, eh?" he said, pointing to the waxwork that looked as if it had been kneaded from pure terror. "It was a little Italian who asked me do it, and although today's artists claim there are no more models, it's simply because they don't know how to see. I met that one in the street one December evening, shivering, gaunt, and almost begging. He took me for an assassin and he was afraid . . . it was his terror that I caught; he was deliciously frightened."

"And what happened to him?" I asked, a little troubled.

"Huh! The same thing that happens to them all when they pose too young and, as children, live in poverty in Paris. I think he died of consumption."

"Are you certain?" I insisted.

"Oh yes, he really is dead. Isn't he, Gormas? Little Antonio Monforti in Beaujon?"

And as Gormas nodded yes, I heard a voice whispering in my ear:

"That is the sort of wax that you need."

Roy Lisker

On Tightropes

From *FERMENT VI*, December 1983

Both absurd and cruel, that audiences demand that the tightrope walker should walk across the high wire without a safety net underneath; for the same skill is involved with or without one. If the acrobat slips and falls, a thrilling experience becomes a horrible tragedy, the moment when the Mass faces itself and sees its own ugliness. But if no safety net is to be used, why keep the line up so high? Why not string it a foot off the ground? Once again, there is no difference in terms of the skill needed to cross it. It is a form of showmanship which has its seat in the mind of the audience itself: height, the sense of danger, fear—and does not life itself often take on the aspect of a tightrope walk for which the wire has been strung needlessly high? One must walk it because below there is the abyss and destruction. But imagine that someone, in protest against the tightrope, should deliberately fall of it to an inevitable and cruel death. Do the others on the tightrope realize the validity of his seemingly insane act? But is it really insane? Does the value of his act lessen the pain of destruction? May it not sometimes *save* him from destruction, or will he always be a mere man, who, because he "slipped", of course fell to his death? Or let us say that he did not die, but was horribly crippled. Does this crippled rebel now have the right to demand special privileges from those on the rope, or are they correct in ignoring him? Yet how else is one to register a protest except through deliberately slipping off the rope?

But this, the greatest agony of all: does rope really exist in the first place? If in fact there is no rope, it is nonetheless true that a cruel destruction awaits those who fall off of it; provided that they see the rope in the first place. If someone is not aware of any tightrope, then there is no dying for him, nor any need to register a protest. Both the protester and the mob appear equally foolish to him. Yet his sympathies will lie more with the protester than with the herd.

W.J. Davies & Paul Griffiths

Constraint and Release

Paul Griffiths talks to W. J. Davies about his Ophelian novels, let me tell you *and* let me go on

Paul Griffiths' *let me tell you* and its sequel, *let me go on,* are based on a deceptively simple premise: they use only the 481 different words Shakespeare gave Ophelia in *Hamlet.* Named "O" here, she has the chance to tell her story on her own terms, first her life before the events of the play, then, more mysteriously, after. Playful and exuberant, these are those rare kinds of experimentations which manage to be both formally inventive and deeply affecting; Harry Mathews described *let me tell you* as "a beautiful and enthralling work, as well as a great success in Oulipian terms." In the play, Ophelia's words are used to mark her descent into madness. In Griffiths' novels, with those same words set to different purposes and rhythms, she finds new ways to describe her inner life, her past and the possible futures that lie ahead.

WJD: I'd like to begin by going back to how you started these novels, Paul. Which came first, Ophelia or the experimental form?

PG: I'd already settled on this idea of writing with a restricted vocabulary, but it didn't take long to decide it should be Ophelia's. Not only is she a sympathetic and enigmatic character of whom we well might want to learn more than we do in the play, she has a vocabulary of just the right size: a little under 500 different words, many of which are archaic or unusual, so that they can't be used too often. Indeed, only about a third of her words are to be found in the core vocabulary of Basic English. So the protagonist of *let me tell you* and *let me go on* has a minimal vocabulary with which to express her thoughts, her feelings, the whole story of her life, and her relationships with other people. She shares the condition we all experience when we can't find words for what we want to say, except that with her that condition is taken to an extreme.

It must have felt extreme at times for you, too, writing a life in that way.

Yes, but before we go any further, I want to say that this limitation, like any such limitation if it's to be useful, is not so much a constraint as a release. It pushes you to find ways round the problem.

The freedom within the limitation. It reminds me of Beckett's description of his decision to write in French instead of English, that he was able to write "without style," which I take to be writing in a way that's free, or more free, of linguistic habits and clichés. There's a crispness and clarity to the prose in your novels because of the restraint.

Thank you. This particular limitation makes it possible to say very simple things freshly, because they have had to go through the sieve, as it were. The narrator of *let me tell you* is aware of the challenge that faces her, but she is also aware of the possibilities. She even starts out, right at the beginning of the first chapter, by bringing it into the open:

> So: now I come to speak. At last. I will tell you all I know. I was deceived to think I could not do this. I have the powers; I take them here. I have the right. I have the means. My words may be poor, but they will have to do.

She doesn't have to refer to this again; from here, her words will speak for themselves.

One of the things she wants her words to do is make connections with others, I think, while remaining herself as well. To be seen and heard and acknowledged as a person among others.

It matters to her, yes. I think it's one of those very simple things her words are able to say so clearly. She has a little soliloquy on "the hand," for example, at the end of which she turns to the reader:

> A hand may be an argument to them that do not believe in love.
>
> "Here is my hand," one will say. "This is my hand. I give you my hand." There's nothing I may give you that means more.
>
> "I take your hand," the other will say. "I have your hand in mine." There's nothing I may take from you that means more. "And in being like that, I have given you my hand. This is my hand.

This is me."

Here: I have held it out to you. Take my hand. Go with me. Be with me.

During the thirteen years I spent writing the book, I found other possibilities raised by working with a restricted vocabulary—and particularly with the Ophelian vocabulary. One example: Ophelia never names herself, so the narrator of my novels can't call herself "Ophelia" but only "O," which puts her at a slight remove from the Shakespeare character. She both is Ophelia and is not; she has a little room for maneuver, which she develops through the first book.

I suppose the majority of us don't go around saying our own names all that often, unless we're introducing ourselves, which Ophelia never has the chance to do.

That's true. The only character Ophelia names is Hamlet—but I don't have her do so in the novels, because Hamlet's presence would be overwhelming. Accordingly, O refers to him only as "the young lord," and his name has to be filtered into the text another way. (I took it as a rule that every word Ophelia speaks, whether in the Second Quarto text or the First Folio, has to make its appearance in *let me tell you*.) O can also talk about her "father" and her "brother," but she doesn't have the word "mother."

An absence that leaves Ophelia more vulnerable to the men in the play, perhaps?

Possibly, but this is where Ophelia and O are not quite the same. For me, a lack became a benefit. If in telling the story of her life O cannot speak of her mother, there must be some reason. Searching for a possible reason led me into territory such as this, where the mother is crowing to her daughter about a threesome:

"To be dupped and dupped again. To be dupped by the one and then by the other, and then by the one again, for as long as it will take that you cannot remember which is which. To have them look and look and find the doors, find all the doors. Call out. More. More. Now. To be gyved. To be jangled. To be larded. To be larded all over and in me. To be done. To be well and truly done."

Not only does this allow me to use some unusual words, and not only does it provide a reason why O shuns even the word "mother," it gives voice to the fulminating understory of frustrated and corrupt sex that's there in the play.

Then, in contrast, we have a scene involving O's first love, whom she cannot name, but whom she can certainly address:

You are my sun. You have sun-blasted me, and turned me to light.

You have made me like glass—like glass in an ecstasy from your light, like glass in which light rained and rained and rained and goes on, like glass in which there are showers of light that cannot end.

Such youthful sentiments! It breathes so much life into her story.

There are other characters in O's tiny, enclosed world, characters made possible by her words, most notably the Polonius family maid. Polonius is a high court official, and so his household would certainly include servants. A maid is plausible; she is also necessary. O's mother being venomous, it is the maid who, in her strength, gives O a sense of home. It's also the maid who reveals to the young O the whole story lying ahead. This was one of the gifts *let me tell you* gave me, to mitigate the long labor: to find that I could, with so few words, produce a tolerable synopsis of the play. That was fun. Here's an example:

"What will truly please him will be the men that come to do a play. He'll know them from before. He'll have one of them redeliver a speech, which your father will not like, but for one of the words.

"He, the young lord as he is by now, will then have them give their play—but with a speech that he's made up for one of them—before the king, the lady and many another: indeed, almost all of you. Not me, as I do not have to say. But you'll be there. This is when you are a young lady. You'll be there, as will he—he'll play with you at the play. With you and with the king. More with the king."

The Ophelian vocabulary, limited as it is, nevertheless has some very useful words: "time," "memory," "remember," "music," "play," "other" and "another," to name a few. At the same time, many simple words are missing, besides "mother." The protagonist of *let me tell you* and *let me go on* is relating an autobiography in which she can never say "I am," so again ways have to be found round this.

Are there any others that stick in the memory?

I found it hard to do without "or." I wanted my central character to have alternatives.

And despite that O uses so many different kinds of speech and writing while telling her story.

I wanted the novels to have as much variety as possible, to counter the restriction; I wanted the text to burst out from its confines. So in *let me tell you* there are songs and sonnets, childhood reminiscences and tales of high misdemeanor, letters (from Polonius abroad) and a play. The Polonius letters allowed in some comedy, which I was glad to have, and which again, of course, accords with the Shakespeare play. The play in the novel does that, too, as a little comedy being rehearsed by O, her father, her brother, and the young lord, with all the release and irritation that come with amateur theatricals. I should say that when other characters speak, whether in the play or as themselves, their words have to occur not only in Ophelian but also in their own vocabularies. There are intersections I found interesting in telling me things about Shakespeare's language in the play. For instance, Ophelia shares "obey" only with Gertrude. Make of that what you will, as I might say in Ophelian.

And they say it respectively to the men who govern their lives, Polonius and Claudius. But "obey" is also said by Hamlet, for example, in Act 1, Scene 2, to Gertrude: "I shall in all my best obey you, madam." I suppose he is making the point of emphatically not saying it to Claudius but to his mother.

Whoops. Yes, of course. Let me check. Indeed, Hamlet says it twice, whether we're looking at the Second Quarto or the First Folio. I suppose I could say that in both Hamlet's usages his mother is the one he will obey, and so Gertrude is there in the immediate context—also that in both there's a high degree of irony. But it would be more honest to admit I slipped up—though it was a productive error: it prompted me to have O make a point of sharing the word with Gertrude.

I'm sure that's not the only mistake in terms of the rules of the game. The first edition of *let me tell you*, published by Reality Street in 2008, failed to include the word "sewing," which of course is in the Ophelian vocabulary:, ". . . as I was sewing in my closet . . ." (Q2), ". . . as I was sewing in my chamber . . ." (F1).

Speaking of the different editions, I let O have all the Ophelian words in both Q2 and F1, in order not to miss words, as in this case, where by doubling up we are allowed both "chamber" and "closet." The case that clinched the decision was another line: "Like sweet bells jangled out of time" (Q2), "Like sweet bells jangled out of tune" (F1). It was really important to have "time," which Ophelia doesn't say anywhere else, and "tune" was useful, too. (A nice coincidence: Gertrude has both words in her speech on Ophelia's death, F1 version: "Which time she chanted snatches of old tunes.")

To come back to Hamlet, I took the decision that in *let me go on* the young lord speaks in the novel only when he's in character in the play rehearsal; I didn't think I could or should make up lines for Hamlet.

I agree. Hamlet recedes further when you take O's story beyond him in let me go on, *freeing her even further.*

Right. In *let me go on*, we've left Hamlet behind, along with all but one of the other characters from the Shakespeare play. Where *let me tell you* was largely narrated in the past tense—though with this small vocabulary, consistency of tense had to be abandoned from time to time—in *let me go on* we follow O in her present as she seeks out what she can now be, having exited her play.

The limitation to Ophelia's words means O's voice is distinctly consistent across both novels, but did you notice as you were writing the sequel a change in how you approached this next part of her story?

Having left Elsinore, we can move further away from the diction of the play. O now moves not so much through time as through space here, in a new landscape where she meets other people who share her situation. Like her, they have kept their original vocabularies, so, like the Shakespeare characters in *let me tell you*, they can use only words that Ophelia also has. And though they have left their plays, they may still be marked by their experiences there. Here, for example, is an important character from *Antony and Cleopatra*:

"There was . . . let's call him a soldier. He's in love. A soldier in love. And there's two he's in love with. A he and a she. And these two are in love with each other. They do not see his love. They are so in tune with each other that for them there's no other music."

Generally speaking, the prose is lighter here, more contemporary. That was partly because I'd had a lot of time with the language, through *let me tell you* and other things, as well as because the original play had been left behind.

At one point, though, it comes back in the person of Ophelia's brother making an attempt to retrieve her:

"I wish I did not have to say this to you—"

"Father. Is he not well?"

"He is well; he is well."

"Go on."

"You remember how he comes to his death?"

"How could I not?"

"With him now it's like it's a true death, like he'll be dead and gone. He goes on with it—you know what he's like—but his heart's not in it now."

O's longest encounter is with her counterpart in the First, so-called "Bad," Quarto: Ofelia—or "O-fie," as she has to call herself. O-fie lives on the top of a mountain (we spend a good bit of time in both books up the mountain or over the mountain, for obvious reasons), and O makes her way up there.

It's a significant moment of companionship and recognition for her.

It is. They tell each other stories, sing songs, compare fashion preferences, or just hang out, basking in their affinity. O-fie has more words than O, and introduces some that O does not have. One or two Ofelian but non-Ophelian words here break the otherwise strict rule that both books are entirely in Ophelian. Perhaps the infringement will signal to O that she should move on. Certainly it causes her a little confusion, as in this dialogue, where O begins:

"Tell me all you may of yourself."

"You'll know it already."

"All what?"

"Already. Like: by now, from before. Already."

"I'll remember."

Eventually, though, O realizes that her quest does not end here, with her second self, and that she must go on to find her first. Further along she has conversations with the captain of a ship going by, the hostess of a pub, a sprite who takes up residence in her head, and an observant Jew who is reading the Psalms, albeit in the King James Version, which was published close in time to *Hamlet* (seven years after the Second Quarto) and duly includes passages in Ophelian:

Many there be which say of my soul,
There is no help for him in God . . .

Her soul is her own, not made up of the judgments of others. So she comes back to a belief that she alone can take her where she needs to go? "I have the right. I have the means."

Exactly. Besides, the inhabitants of this fairytale world are often too caught up in their own dramas to offer the protagonist any advice or assistance; think of the two young women who speak at the same time and squabble. Some, though, treat her with more compassion and steer her in the direction of the one they believe will answer her needs: the Master.

Yet though her final encounter is not with some magus, she does end the book, as she did *let me tell you*, at a point where an altogether new realm of existence seems to be opening up for her.

Will she again cross the threshold?

For now, the question is left in the reader's hands.

let me tell you and let me go on are published by Henningham Family Press in the UK and available in the US in a combined edition, published by New York Review Books.

REVIEW | Kevin Davey

let me tell you and *let me go on*
Paul Griffiths
New York Review Books, April 2025

She appears on stage five times only. An innocent, she's vulnerable. Men carve out the path she walks until her lover dumps her and her father is killed. Traumatised, she takes her own life, or is drowned accidentally. Shakespeare rigs an open verdict.

Ophelia's pre-scripted life, all downhill from the start, has long attracted feminist readings and retellings—from Elaine Showalter's pioneering rethink in the 1980s to Lisa Klein's radical revision of her life for teenage girls—which celebrate the trampled 'rose of May' as a figure of resistance.

In *Let Me Tell You* and *Let Me Go On*, Paul Griffiths draws on the metafictional energies of Becket, Borges and Calvino—a pivotal trio who stretched storytelling in unprecedented directions—to deepen and further extend Ophelia's recovery.

Griffiths empowers Ophelia to speak for a second and third time, voicing—in her own words—a raw, disturbing prequel and a spine-tingling sequel to the last few weeks of her life glimpsed in Hamlet. Griffiths identifies 483 words spoken by Ophelia in the Second Quarto and First Folio editions and the revivified narrator speaks with those alone.

It's reasonable to expect that a limited, self-denying lexicon will quickly become monotonous, crude and clumsy, and unable to deliver nuance and subtlety. The fewer the words, the greater the tongue-tied dullness, surely? Force-fitted phrases will mask events. One can hear the objections: isn't writing in this way merely mosaic making—or perhaps plumbing, as Ballard once described William Burrough's use of cut-ups.

Not here, not in the virtuoso hands of Paul Griffiths. His Ophelian monologues recast and add fresh mystery to a tragedy most of us think we know. A nuncannily familiar voice unfolds; a reconstellation of Ophelia, perhaps of Hamlet as a whole, is set in motion. From the opening lines a tension between received language and the act of speaking is foregrounded as central: "So now I come to speak. At last. I will tell you all I know. I was deceived to think that I could not do this." Uncluttered storytelling, small differences, creative recombinations and new disclosures follow. Surprise and insight accumulate. An intertextual polyphony—words which were expected, and some which were not, all resonating with remembered readings, and half-recalled performances—soon sounds from the page.

Don't be surprised this is so. Have you forgotten how, as children, we thrilled to Green Eggs and Ham, in which Dr Seuss riffed quickfire, wondrous comic changes from only fifty words? Permutational performance is an adult pleasure too— in poetry, where it is fundamental to the villanelle and sestina, for example, or in the French nouveau roman, most notably in Robbe-Grillet and Claude Simon's repetitions intensified by variation.

In these paradoxical monologues, Ophelia reworks her script and finds fresh voice, much changed yet much the same. She is no longer passive: "I have come to see that my path up to now was a path made for me—and it could go on. I do not like it, and I will not take it. More and more I know where it goes." In Let Me Tell You she is prescient about the limitations and restricted choices which lay ahead in the play, mirroring but also contrasting with her author, whose constraints are voluntary and options more numerous. Griffiths' Ophelia knows she is rooted in relations of language and power, and that she will remain enmeshed within them. She is clearly a fiction. A troubling question arises: is the reader too? An unusually self-aware reading experience—more alert to one's literary endowments, to echoes and returns, to absences and other possibilities—indeed to our shaping by writing—ensues.

Some of the unsayables are revealing. Famously, Ophelia was never given the word mother by Shakespeare. To backfill the gap a remote and forbidding "she", "the lady", "the other one" is assembled. She was an unloved, neglected child. Ophelia's subjectivity is transformed.

Because 'said' is also missing from her lexicon, tenses become mysterious. Reported speech becomes tantalisingly conditional, habitual, or imperative: she would say, he had to say. Why? New questions arise.

This circling, recycled voice realises it has limited free will and agency. Friends tell her "My tongue is not my own." At the same time she has a renewed sense of possibility, parallel to that of the author: "What should I do? Which path should I take? This way, that way?"

This sense of contingency—that everything might be otherwise, and can be made so, while recognisably persisting—is what propels much of Griffiths' fiction, from his first novel *Myself and Marco Polo* (1989), subtitled 'a novel of changes', in which a cellmate of the celebrated Silk Road traveller becomes his ghostwriter. As the two bunkies quarrel about art, religion and philosophy—broaching the issue of whether "infinite alternatives must be countenanced as a part of reality"—Rustichello fakes and fabricates much of the famous fourteenth century memoir.

The Lay of Sir Tristram (1991) took the legend of Tristan and Iseult back to basics—a woman weeping, a boy on the shore—reopening the story's possibilities with inversions and reversals, other tellings and critique: "He is back on land, but different land . . . This is a story about a boy weeping, a weeping boy. No. He is walking gaily along a woodland path." Headings include: "VII. A problem, with four possible solutions", an episode in which each paragraph offers an alternative to its precedent.

Mr Beethoven (2020) was a counterfactual game of what-iffery in which the composer was sent to a country he never visited to compose an oratorio he never wrote. The mode was closer to traditional historical fiction than his previous work, and gently buttressed with social and psychological realism, but Beethoven's words were all selected from documentary sources, and the narrative voice, true to form, considered changes in direction and focus as it unfurled.

The Ophelian texts relinquish the realist safety rail. They are less tessellated and likely to unravel at any moment than the early novels. They are also, in places, surreal. At one point, make-do ingredients generate a mouth-watering menu which includes "Valentine's Eyes", "Heart of Owl with rose honey" and "Twice Turned Shoulder of Young Robin." Memorable metaphors are struck from what's to hand: "That mountain: it was a green sandal loosed from heaven." Having no access to 'toes', Ophelia may not tiptoe: she walks "heels raised up as we go", an awkwardness enhanced by scarcity.

As no other hue is available, the palette contracts to green. Griffiths thrives on such shortages. On a games board "one of you must play green, the other the other." That may irritate some readers but the workarounds usually combine comedy and insight. It's one of many ways in which the voluntary constraint upon the writer becomes palpable and shared, a pleasure for the reader too. Anachronisms pile on the fun: who knew Ophelia had a Beatles song within her, and the first draft of the pop ballad Delilah?

The song-bursts are significant. The author is associated with Oulipo, an evolving troupe of writers who deploy strict rules to generate and shape texts. I suspect this isn't the main, or only, driver of his choices. Griffiths is a distinguished authority on contemporary classical music. Music informs his writing practice. We are being led astray when Ophelia informs us "If you wish to have music, you must tear yourself away and go from here."

One can, as it happens, 'go from here' to a Hans Abrahamsen song cycle in which the aurally dazzling soprano Barbara Hannigan sings a variant of the *Let Me Tell You* (Winter and Winter 9102322, 2016). I strongly recommend you do. And lend an ear to Griffiths himself, reading an early draft of the text accompanied by the acclaimed two-bow cellist Frances-Marie Uitti on *There is Still Time* (ECM New Series 1882, 2004)

Luciano Berio's opera *A King Listening*, with its non-linear libretto by Calvino, is an obvious forebear. An isolated and declining ruler—Shakespeare's Prospero reimagined as a theatre director—hears despair being voiced in his palace, along with rehearsals for a performance of *The Tempest*. Messaien's limited transpositions foreshadow Griffiths' rearrangements, as does the formula composition used by Stockhausen for his avant-garde opera *Donnerstag*, and Cage's prepared and constrained pianos. But I am most reminded of the copresence of music and text in some medieval monastic choirs, where the meditative singing of as many as three doctrinal texts at the same time took place. Might this sung sharing and overlaying and repatterning of valued texts have had something in common with our experience of reading Ophelian, or *Myself and Marco Polo* or *The Lay of Tristram* with the original in mind?

Quite possibly. For overlay, simultaneity and intersections between texts are a focus of *The Tomb Guardians* (2021) which was published in England between the two Ophelian texts. Two conversations about the night Jesus left his burial chamber, separated by two millenia, are interpolated. In one, a pair discuss paintings of men believed to be the sentries by the tomb. In the other, the guardians themselves debate the events of the night: sleeping while on duty, the disappearance of one of their number, the rolling away of the stone, possible punishment. Both discussions throw light on the biblical story and puzzles it contains. The fun lays in the jump cuts between the two conversations. Lines from one are transposed or echoed in the other; often the dialogues appear to merge or reply to one another; sometimes the first line of a resumed conversation provides the unspoken thought of the last speaker. The switches and slippages can be unnerving, and are often comic. They dispel any sense of a non-fictional presence. In place of plots and arcs, of parallels and probability, unexpected trapdoors drop and trip the reader from one baffled exchange to another. In no time at all we read "heels raised up as we go."

Games need rules. Griffiths uses them to restore play and choice to writing, and alert questioning to reading. We're reminded that the novel is contingent, always on the road, and need never remain where it is. *Let Me Tell You* and *Let Me Go On* are air drops of inspiration, no less, into our literary logjam.

REVIEW | David Rose

For the Fallen

Human Wishes / Enemy Combatant
Edmond Caldwell
Grand Iota, 2022 (second edition)

I n 2022 a small UK press performed the small miracle of literary resurrection: they republished a novel whose author had been dead for five years and whose original publisher was also defunct, leaving his novel out of print—the literary equivalent of the Biblical Second Death. Sadly, there wasn't the same interest in this as there was for that of Lazarus, with no reviews that I can ascertain in America and only one in Britain.

The miracle-working press was *Grand Iota*, a two-man outfit that punches well above its weight in publishing new fiction and republishing significant out-of-print American novels, including Fanny Howe's *Bronte Wilde* and Barbara Guest's *Seeking Air*; they have also more recently republished an important collection of essays by Eric Mottram, a pioneer of American Studies in Britain—*Blood on the Nash Ambassador*.

I had some small involvement in that republication; my account of it is intended as a be-lated tribute to Edmond—whose non-existence in the world I still haven't adjusted to.

When my first novel, *Vault*, was published, Edmond, whom I didn't know then, saw reference to it somewhere, read it and blogged about it, then sought me out on Facebook. We became friends but also fellow warriors; he told me that what drew him to my novel was its subtitle—*an anti-novel*; he told me that the chutzpah in that, a sure-fire way to turn readers away, was what had drawn him to it.

I later found out when Edmond's first novel was published a year later, that his interest stemmed from the fact that that novel too was an anti-novel, more complicated, more ambitious, wittier than mine. I admit that I had initially bought it as a return of favour, but once I started reading it, I was overwhelmed with admiration—and not a little jealousy. I reviewed it three times: on Amazon.com; on the now extinct, I believe, *Bicycle Review*; then in *American Book Review*.

We remained friends for some years, although there were hiatuses in that online relationship. Edmond would periodically withdraw from Facebook and our contact became sporadic. So when his final withdrawal dragged on and we lost radio contact, I wasn't at first concerned—he would turn up again in his own time.

Sadly, he didn't. It wasn't until some years later that I learnt of his death in 2017, and then the demise of his publisher and disappearance of his novel.

Having become acquainted with *Grand Iota* and its list, indeed read several of its titles, I approached them with the idea of reissuing that novel, having by marvellous coincidence obtained the text as a pdf. from another friend of Edmond's, Steven Augustine—from whose blog I learnt of his death, and who, like me, had loaned out his copy and not had it returned but managed to acquire that pdf.replacement.

To their eternal credit, Ken Edwards and Brian Marley, a.k.a *Grand Iota,* needed little persuasion, seeing immediately the quality of the novel. They published it with an Afterword by Joe Ramsey; a monochrome version of the original, very witty, back cover alongside it; and a superb new front cover for this edition.

However, in writing this tribute, to both Edmond and *Grand Iota,* I decided to do some republishing of my own—what follows is the text of one of my original reviews, that which appeared in *American Book Review* (Vol. 33, no. 5), reproduced with the kind permission of Jeffrey Di Leo.

This was for several reasons: to convey my early response to the novel in its freshness, unclouded by the melancholia arising from the knowledge of Edmond's death (which makes more poignant the final hopeful paragraph), and to pay tribute also to the small press which first took the risk of publishing *Human Wishes/ Enemy Combatant—Say It With Stones.*

Say It With Stones/Interbirth Books are a small, Dallas-based press publishing mainly poetry; *Human Wishes/Enemy Combatant* is their first venture into the novel. They are to be commended on their enterprise and audacity no less than Caldwell himself. This is a witty addition to the ranks of the Postmodernist anti-novel.

But "anti-novel" is an over-used and imprecise term. Let's use the term "novel-in-negative"—less snap but more precision.

Human Wishes proceeds by systematically breaking the rules, confounding the expectations of the novel—plot, character, background setting—so that what we are left with is a novel in reverse.

The rationale for this is given within the text: "If you were to write a truly 'realistic' novel it would have to include these histories of lives in labor and labor in lives, each novel would have to be an endless *roman fleuve* of these loops and strata, each novel a failure because it could not possibly encompass it all, each novel necessarily a fragment and a failure . . ." (p. 129). And to create "rounded" characters depends entirely on such infinitely regressing loops of back-story; on the appearance of psychological depth and temporal depth together causing the effect of realism, because "people just don't go around doing shit for no reason that's not realistic, but if they don't do anything at all it won't be dramatic, if for example they just wander round in circles trapped inside various non-places such as airport baggage-claim terminals and highway rest stops it wouldn't be dramatic, you've got to be realistic yet dramatic . . ." (p. 159).

So here, in place of plot we have structure, and as reinforcement of the structure, a series of (very funny) running gags. The book is in three parts, each of three chapters. They all function discretely, and are all set in just those "non-places", "In-Between Places" Caldwell warns against: airport terminal, Parisian hotel complex for "bumped" passengers, the tourist sites of St. Petersburg, rest-stop, shopping mall, art gallery . . .

This last also functions as a brilliant *mise en abyme*—the gallery is showing an exhibition of Joseph Cornell boxes, those still-lifescapes conjuring a universe in a peep-box. The chapters of *Human Wishes* work the same way, with a cumulative effect.

It also introduces one of the funniest running gags, featuring a constantly metamorphosing James Wood, the literary critic who is, to my amusement, taken very seriously in America (as he is not in Britain). In fact, the principle of Kafkaesque metamorphosis is at the heart of the book, as themes and settings darken.

For instance, the sixth chapter, "Time And Motion", is set in a shopping mall bookshop, a B. Dalton bookshop in fact, an extended meditation on Taylorism, the "scientific" basis of industrial (and literary?) production, written in the style of Thomas Bernhard, and every bit as funny and acidulous. It plays with the possibility of

Taylor's book *The Principles of Scientific Management* turning out to be a parody, an anti-novel in the form of a spoof scientific study. But in passing, it relates Taylorism to the efficiency of the Nazi Holocaust. This is not gratuitous. It links subliminally with a later chapter, a backstory of sorts, although not the realist type Caldwell has dismissed, set in Lydda during the Israeli "cleansing" of 1948.

This in turn, by means of a searing image of a mutely screaming shell-shocked woman, morphs into an elaborate playscript involving Dr. Johnson, his cat, the ubiquitous James Wood, and an early, lost play by Samuel Beckett—*Human Wishes.* Thus is explained the first part of the title.

The second, *Enemy Combatant,* is prepared by another running gag—the (anti-)hero's "facial dismorphia", his obsessive worry over his appearance. Although of Portuguese-American descent, he is convinced he looks Semitic, either Jewish or, more worryingly, Arabic, equally convinced he will end up being arrested as not just a literary terrorist, intent on "blowing up the novel from within", but a real, honest-to-goodness, Al Qaeda-type terrorist, an enemy combatant.

This "facial dismorphia" is, then, more than a trope for fluidity of character in place of Realism's "rounded" character. It is the last and crucial metamorphosis of the book. The final chapter, *Enemy Combatant,* starts fittingly with a parodic reference to Kafka's *Metamorphosis.* And as Kafka's parables turned to chilling literalism under the Nazis—a whole people turned overnight into "vermin"—so the antihero's dismorphic worries become real, or apparently so, when he is indeed arrested and interrogated as possible enemy combatant, during which the past scenes of his life/the book return and coalesce into Kafkaesque nightmare; a haunting *tour de force* to close the book.

It is not, though, despite that nightmare ending, a sombre book; on the contrary, it is bracingly literary in its references, and above all very funny in its wit and linguistic invention. No synopsis could adequately describe it, and this review doesn't attempt to do so. It attempts only to encourage you to read it, slowly, enjoy the ride, and congratulate yourselves on being among the first to recognize the authority of a writer we will all be hearing much more about in the future.

REVIEW | Charles Holdefer

A Black Doe in the Anthropocene
Artress Bethany White
University Press of Kentucky, 2025

Making history isn't only a matter of doing something. It's also the act of *telling* something, constructing a narrative about the past that informs the present. In her latest collection of poetry, *A Black Doe in the Anthropocene,* Artress Bethany White draws on her family history, particularly the enslavement of her ancestors in Virginia and North Carolina, and in unearthing their story she recounts a broader story of African diaspora.

The section entitled "Original Sin" opens with an erasure poem called "A Family History," which begins

"(In the 1700s, a Scottish immigrant) ~~made his~~
~~way to the~~
~~shores of British America and~~ (began) ~~the process~~
~~of~~ (purchasing)
~~land and slaves, to build~~ (a plantation empire).
(This family), ~~with~~
~~the~~
~~surname~~ (Hairston), ~~would establish a practice of~~
~~their slaves not~~
~~regularly being sold outside the family. As a~~
~~result,~~ (both white and
Black)" . . .

What is going on here? The crossed-out words, which recall the tone of a textbook description, appear to attenuate or obfuscate the circumstances. (The reference to keeping the enslaved in the family is explored later in the book.) Here the poet is announcing, in effect, both a politics and an aesthetic. White is not only observing, but seeing *through*.

Some of the most trenchant poems in *A Black Doe* are, in fact, acts of reading. In "A Creased Page from a Hairston Plantation Ledger," the speaker considers a list of humans for sale, a sort of grisly menu, and she wonders at variations in price:

"Today I sift through the names of thirty enslaved
and pause over the sum of $1,000
to see what I imagine a planter might see:
a Black man full of genetic seed
and future saleable progeny.
No wait, it's the price of *John[s] Daughter*,
zeros now plain as lust's desire."

Of all the names mentioned in the poem, "*John[s] daughter*" is the most expensive, costing more, for instance, than *Sam $650* or even *Bill Bradley $850* ("Not everyone / has this last name or a price so high; / it may be literacy or some other skilled pedigree.") Although this daughter doesn't even possess a first name in the ledger, she must possess something else to justify the price. Supply and demand, for the enslaver, is a hermetic affair, placing a high value on the dispensation to rape.

White returns repeatedly to this reality. In "Oral Slave Narrative," she recounts how a family's oral history is sanitized for childish ears, "unsure how babies were made." Avoiding the subject of rape might be understandable in conversations with the very young, but the poem underlines how this avoidance has infiltrated the consciousness of adults, and infantilized the understanding of history and of personal identity.

Reading *A Black Doe*, I thought of my history textbooks in secondary school. I recall that the descriptions of slavery were sober, brief, and without any mention of systemic rape. Actually, what made the biggest impression on me wasn't the text but rather a diagram of a slave ship and the horrific claustrophobic conditions of the Middle Passage. Once I'd seen it, I couldn't unsee it.

White accomplishes something similar here in regard to sexual abuse. Once seen, you cannot unsee it. Of course, this subject is not really "news"—White places an epigraph from Harriet Jacobs' 1861 *Incidents in the Life of a Slave Girl: Written by Herself* at the beginning of the book, which addresses the subject head on. But averting eyes has become an ingrained cultural habit, one that persists to this day.

In another poem about reading, "An Extant Slave Receipt Signed Peter Hairston," she considers a receipt dated 1777 for an ancestor who is namelessly described as a "*Negro wench and child*" and ruefully remarks,

"It is not enough that the sweat of the planter seller
is mixing with the DNA of my fingertips

as his genetic code resides within me.
My inheritance the oft-turned phrase

This family had a habit of not selling off their slaves
and so many receipts neatly tucked away."

Something very similar to this "oft-turned phrase" was crossed out in the poem cited earlier, "A Family History." References to the family's "habit" or "practice" are rather euphemistic—is there even an implied paternal benevolence there?—instead of a recognition of the use of women for forced sex or as "breeders."

Formally speaking, most of *A Black Doe* is written in free verse, with occasional rhymes reflecting speech patterns. It also includes nocturne, aubade, and a sharply observed ghazal entitled "Runners," dedicated to Ahmaud Arbery. The text of "Runaway Slave Affidavit Dated March 1831" is an interesting experiment in found poetry, where White inserts line breaks into a document submitted to a Virginia magistrate and renders the legalistic language in short bursts of free verse. It's an astute choice, as the blank space on the page actually makes the procedural brutality more stark.

At first I thought *A Black Doe in the Anthropocene* was an unwieldy title, but upon finishing the book, it seems apt. The historical scope here is vast, and frankly, not easy to parse within the confines of a review. I've referred mainly to poems about slavery, which is central to the collection, but White also writes about emigration to Liberia, Reconstruction, contemporary Ghana and recent atrocity in Charlottesville, among other subjects. This is both a work of scrupulous research and a chronicle of White's own experiences in the glare of recent events.

A Black Doe in the Anthropocene is unflinching, ambitious work, a distillation of historical consciousness into poetry.

Massive Massive Oil Slick
Sean Ashton
Ma Bibliotheque, 2025

The subdued cover image of Sean Ashton's new para novel *Massive Massive Oil Slick* (2025) conveys a disquieting sense of identity crisis via the schizophrenic architectural ensemble of a neo-vernacular Barratt style home, accented by mock Tudor half timbering, a Georgianised front porch and what appear to be 1970s-style office windows. Then there's the tautophony of its title. What is going on here? Well, Ashton's book is an OuLiPean lite exercise: procedural writing with its outcomes on display. Why para though? Mainly because *MMOS* has the look and thickness of a short literary novel, but is constrained, rather than say *Finnegans Wake* which is totally unrestrained, and a prolonged language orgy. No, here we have controlled scripting, deracinated sentences minus jouissance that audit a world gone wrong, gone bad: post-imperial Britain, very much shorn of its historical prefix 'Great', a case of managed decline, dysfunction. *MMOS*'s suave plotlessness is also an attribute that situates it outside of, and indeed beyond the scope of the conventional, narrative-driven romance, spy thriller or mystery tale; a foreign import from the art world but with ambitions way beyond that perimeter fence.

Despite being set up as a monologue, *MMOS* is never a bore, its weave of paragraphs delimited by three main *incipits*, i.e. 'Expect' (predictive/fateful), 'Suppose' (speculative/theoretical) and 'Avoid' (minatory/experiential) which stem, and pour out from the speaker's physiological 'cockpit', in an inglorious slick (the titular word is well chosen), sometimes recursive, crazily accumulative, but propelled by Ashton's angst and sorrow, that seizes on the horrifying banalities and vexations of everyday subjective life in 2025. 'Expect' has been lifted, as if from BBC 'Countryfile's' tweedified weekly weather forecast or regular roadside traffic updates, and emphasises impasses, delays, jams, while occasionally lingering over social phenomena that are slowly vanishing, such as sandwich boards and belisha beacons! So Sean from Accounts is very much a mock conservative, trying on old fogey carpet slippers, resigned to the passing of heritage from the pre Covid-19 world

> *baking hot phone boxes smelling of piss gone*
> there being
> *no stable zeitgeist any more, no collective memory*

yet with his bad boy's tongue lodged firmly in his cheek. In one hilarious episode a builder arrives in order to service Dante's *Inferno* a subterranean portal to which, happens to be placed directly under the speaker's dwelling (that crazy Barratt-style home again), and in a rare moment of interaction with an other, declares in a catchphrase that 'it's all going to have to come out', showing Ashton's attunement to colloquial parlance, for *MMOS* is an unrelenting catalogue of the faded, dead and dying, pop culture piledriven hard into the highbrow. Another of his anchor points is the lament 'all over, all over, all over', as if Michel de Montaigne had been reincarnated and was attempting elegiacally, under the influence of Kenneth Goldsmith's rigid ploys, to grasp the complexity and sheer bulk of digital data in cyberspace; for a lot of this para novel emanates from the online world, meaning it is truly a warped dystopian vision; although its literary antecedents could plausibly include St Augustine's *Confessions*, Daniel Defoe's *A Journal of the Plague Year* and Fyodor Dostoyevsky's *Notes from Underground*. Yet this strangely gripping, Hudibrastic text, poses some serious questions about traditional form (especially how it has been altered beyond recognition by formatting), and more importantly even the bothersome need to conjure up or devise the imaginary—fiction in other words—when the nature of contemporary reality is so disturbing, grotesque and comical? Thus Ashton figures as streetwise rapporteur, rather than straight novelist, his post-Cartesian mind disintegrating into gaga at times, under extreme pressure (that reiterated *Massive* of the title betraying how experience can just be too big for extra, fancier words, and so must be dealt with as if a child were placing one identical wooden brick upon another), yet somehow, just somehow, still hanging on to the art of writing as his coping mechanism, his salvation, another feature that makes *MMOS* so appealing: its tirades offer viral immunity, a prophylactic to the bombarded reader, sick with fear and loathing, incapable of finding words adequate to such a monstrous global reality.

Ashton has confessed to me that he still largely (i.e. 60%) writes as a reader, and that his fans understand *MMOS* better than he does; but his labours do prepare us for a great post-human shift, by listing the bygone and antiquated curatorially, a dilemma which Madeleine Thien, in a recent *Times Literary Supplement* survey, summed up as 'a double helix: what must we preserve against catastrophe and against oblivion for the future?' Bathetically this includes such benchmark moments as the sugary sweets Opal Fruits being rebranded as Starburst. Zut alors! Come what may though, Ashton's merry slick just goes on and on, as if conspiracy theory, memoir, self-help paperbacks and autofiction were being sucked in, melted down and deformed, then made newly resplendent as one metaphysically coherent hellscape? And right on time, deep into the book, a section is dedicated to a hell-themed tourist attraction, which seems to be a literary cousin of the Chapman brothers monumental installation *Fucking Hell* (2008), an upended, FUBAR-ed world. Yet, although *MMOS* is grimly diagnostic of human self-inflicted ailments and folly, it is also a hilarious romp, and offers an unrelenting critique and takedown of the 1% of oligarchs too, those shadowy power brokers now running things that is, who in the near, very near future can expect to suffer citizen justice 'stone-blind, groping along on all fours like Nebuchadnezzar'.

Lastly, as a final page, the book comes with its own Playlist of relevant tunes, ranging from northern soul to obscure punk, and acid house. On its YouTube page the cited New Fast Automatic Daffodils track 'Big' is commented on by @Mothbeatl: 'My goodness me! what a veritable banger it is!' The same could be said of Sean Ashton's *MMOS*, less a book than a menacing entity which has escaped its soft covers.

CHRISTOPHER BOUCHER

The Book
and the Sea

It had been a trying summer for Issue 18 of *Exacting Clam*—one full of extensive revisions and difficult edits—so that fall the issue booked an appointment with a therapist. One rainy afternoon in September, the book-in-progress sat down on a leather chair across from an elderly man who held a cup of hot tea in both hands. The therapist took a small sip and said, "Why don't you tell me what brings you here?"

"It's been a rough few months," the issue confessed.

"Rough in what way?" said the therapist.

The literary journal tried to explain his predicament— the edits, the cover selection.

"I'm not hearing anything out of the ordinary here," the therapist said. "You want a good cover, don't you?"

"Sure, but . . ." The book leaned forward in his chair. "Here it is: I don't know what I'm for—what I *am*."

The therapist looked bemused. "You're a literary journal."

"But what's *that*, exactly? 'Wintered air, unclaimed in the cellar reeking of rhubarb wine—'"

"Yes," said the therapist, "but also—"

"'Peplos made of leaves and a himation made of coarse grasses'? 'A poet embroiled in many a heated discussion'?

"My identity is not fully understood," Issue 18 added.

"But aren't you just about to be published?" The therapist was having some comprehension difficulty. "To be *born*, as it were?"

"'Publishing is Murder,'" said the issue. The therapist shook his head in confusion. "That's one of my reviews," the issue continued. "'Publishing Is Murder: A True Crime Book Review.'" "And that review," said the therapist, "and your other work, will soon be read! Isn't that exciting?"

"Sure," said the issue. "But then what? There'll be other issues, right? Issue nineteen, issue twenty. Issue twenty-five?"

"So what are you proposing?" asked the therapist, smiling weakly. "That you be the *only* issue of—"

"Of course not," said the book. "But what makes me different? What makes me *me*?"

The doctor diagnosed Issue 18 with acute anxiety and prescribed it some literary medication.

Later that night, the issue went out with some friends—*Exacting Clam 10* and the newest issues of *Granta* and *The Paris Review*—to get a few drinks and shoot some pool. "Dude, it's going to be OK," assured *The Paris Review* as they sat in their corner booth. "It's not like you're not the first journal to feel this way."

"What meds did they prescribe you?" asked *Granta*.

"Me, I was always afraid," said *The Paris Review*. "It makes you wonder."

"What meds?" *Granta* asked again.

"An LSSRI—I don't remember the name of it." Issue 18 stared into his full glass of beer.

"*L* SSRI?" asked *The Paris Review*.

"It's a literary selective serotonin—"

"The drops close together all over the pane," mumbled *Granta*.

"Come on, man," *The Paris Review* said, punching Issue 18 lightly. "Look at *Clam* Ten! He's doing fine, right?"

"Every conversation is a condition to be explained," shouted *Exacting Clam 10* from the pool table, where he was preparing to take a shot. He took it, missed, and winced. ". . . Kafka's observation that 'A book must be the axe for the frozen sea within us.'"

"I was not drunk and I was not sober," *Granta* hollered from a stool in the corner.

"Know what I think you need?" said *The Paris Review* to Issue 18. "A vacation. Get away for a few days. Quiet down all the noise, you know?"

"That's actually not a bad idea," Issue 18 said. And that's exactly what he did: he found an AirBnB in Provincetown later that night and drove out to Cape Cod the next afternoon. After checking into his place, the issue walked down Commercial Street, treated himself to a good dinner, and fell asleep early. The next morning he was awake at 5 a.m. and out on the beach by first light. As the sun rose over the water, the book stood in the wet sand and let the waves lap the footers of his pages. Issue 18 had always loved the ocean—the rushy rhythm of the waves, the boats rocking gently in place.

Good morning, the book said to the sea.

The sea looked back at *Exacting Clam 18*, but didn't say anything.

Can I ask you a question? said the issue.

The sea shrugged and said, Shoot.

I've been trying to—this sounds dumb—understand myself, the book said. What I'm for.

What you're *for*? the sea said.

You, the book continued, you're full of life—

OK, said the sea, but—

Me, I'm just a single issue, said the book.

Yeah but, it's the same thing, the sea said. You see that, right?

It isn't at all, said the book. I'm just an unrelenting catalogue of the faded, dead and dying, pop culture piledriven hard into the highbrow.

And—what else?

The book looked inside himself, read his own pages. Then he said, A stadium is ancient architecture for containing and apportioning fantasy.

And?

I am karaoke.

The sea smiled.

A world of lush green leaves and plants, said the book. A world where butterflies fluttered, danced, and pirouetted with magnetic charm.

See? the ocean said. A *world* of lush green leaves. A *world*.

Something settled inside Issue 18, like words affixing to a page. The book thanked the sea, turned back to the sand, walked up to his car and drove home.

Mike Silverton

More Enduring Than a Diamond

A poem more enduring than a diamond?
Impossible but yes!
In our exuberance we pour hair on our wine,
cascading o'er the flesh shielding our coccyges
from scrutiny. So! A first in life and art!
Almost hairy coccyges!

The best poems smell of faraway caraway.
They mesmerize constituencies, yet beauty goes rancid
too long in the sun, so enable your resolve
with a good breakfast,
the day's most important meal.

The best poems inspire envy. Swinburne vivifies, enfeebled,
sod-flecked, malodorous, in chunks. Also
I think we must pause and kiss.

The best poems throw switches somewhat recklessly,
allowing hummingbirds of a vaguely threatening demeanor to
menace ornithologists. While no one seems to care,
indifference offers no impediment to a courier, breathless,
with a fresh line:

"A moist aroma upside-down . . . !"
Somewhere that could be interesting,
plus thoughts about skin-care,
plus entertaining directions to alternative routes.
"Where should I put this Friend of Music?"
"Volta! Gas! I love you! Alas!"
For a better view of the poet's aspects
one removes a thick black impasto. In his
melancholy phase (see phases of the moon)
the poet fills sauce pans with tears, their specific gravity
exceeding that of urine. "Is that a consommé?"
No, nor a contumely, mostly, and O how the blood
it makes one to dance in and out of
holes in the air!

Time is odorless. If one values his place in
the Cabaret Voltaire's Catalog of Heirs,
one avoids adding thyme to our syllabic goulash.
Better than average poets experience time as a textured surface.
For the very best poets time is like a mango juice spill one
forgot to wipe up. Not to neglect the auditory. If one
knows how to listen, one would have heard
the very best poet ripening:

In infancy, squeaks; in adolescence,
rumblings; in maturity, ruffles
and flourishes.

Impossible but yes!

Contributors

Emily Adams-Aucoin is published in literary magazines such as Electric Literature's *The Commuter, Identity Theory, Sixth Finch, North American Review*, and *Colorado Review*. She's a poetry editor for *Kitchen Table Quarterly*.

Stephen Bett is a widely and internationally published Canadian poet. His two most recent books are *Broken Glosa* (Chax Press, 2023) and *SongBu®st* (BlazeVOX, 2024).

Laurie Blauner's flash fiction has appeared in *The Cincinnati Review, The Laurel Review, The Rupture, The Best Small Fictions*, and *New World Writing* among other magazines. Her second hybrid nonfiction book, *Swerve*, was just released from Rain Mountain Press. A recent novel is available from Spuyten Duyvil Press. Her latest poetry book, *Come Closer*, won the Library of Poetry Award from Bitter Oleander Press. She lives in Seattle, Washington.

P.J. Blumenthal, an American writer in Munich, Germany, writes in both German and English. He is the author of *Winston Hewlett's Impotence* (Sagging Meniscus, 2024), a non-fiction book on feral man, *Kaspar Hausers Geschwister* (Kaspar Hauser's Siblings), and a German-language blog, "Der Sprachbloggeur."

Christopher Boucher is the author of the novels *How to Keep Your Volkswagen Alive* (Melville House, 2011), *Golden Delicious* (MH, 2016), and *Big Giant Floating Head* (MH, 2019). He teaches writing and literature at Boston College and is Managing Editor of *Post Road Magazine*.

Marvin Cohen (1931–2025) was the author of many novels, plays, and collections of essays, stories, and poems. He lived on the Lower East Side of Manhattan.

Kevin Davey is the author of *English Imaginaries*, an account of the transformation of Englishness in the twentieth century (2000). As a director of The Innovatory he mentored a large number of creative businesses in London before writing a trilogy of experimental fictions: *Playing Possum* (2017), *Radio Joan* (2020) and *Toothpull of St Dunstan* (2025), all published by Aaaargh! Press. These texts engage with turning points in English history, using peripheral spaces as a constraint, and twentieth century modernism—particularly Eliot, Pound, and Khlebnikov—as a compass.

W.J. Davies' essays and reviews can be found in *Literary Review, Review 31, Slightly Foxed* and elsewhere. His story 'Pest Problem' is included in Brilliant Flash Fiction's 2024 anthology, and he has been shortlisted for a Cranked Anvil fiction prize. He lives in South East England.

R.J. Dent is a poet, novelist, essayist and translator. He has written three novels, a book-length study of Emily Dickinson's poetry and a true crime book about Blanche Monnier. He has also translated several European classics into English, including works by Baudelaire, Sade, Lautréamont, Jarry, Breton, Louÿs, Artaud, Crevel and Éluard. His website is www.rjdent.com

Noah Drauschak was trained in poetry at Lafayette College & Temple University. He lives in Philadelphia with his fiancée and a demon cat called St. Ray. He is presently writing a collection of poetic fables elaborating on the traditions of Marie de France, Kafka, Schopenhauer, Borges, and many others. His work has also appeared in *The Gargoyle*.

Gregory Feeley's first novel, *The Oxygen Barons*, was nominated for the Philip K. Dick Award. He has published two subsequent novels, *Arabian Wine* and *Kentauros*, and his short fiction has been frequently anthologized in Year's Best volumes and twice nominated for the Nebula Award. His nonfiction has appeared in the *New York Times Magazine*, the *Times Literary Supplement*, the *Washington Post*, *The Atlantic Monthly*, *USA Today*, and numerous literary quarterlies. Two portions of a novel, *Neptune's Reach*, have appeared in Year's Best anthologies this year with a third to appear this fall from *Asimov's Science Fiction*. A longtime college instructor in English, he has recently returned to full-time writing.

Tom Formaro is a writer, drummer, and dad. His poetry has appeared in *Janus Head, Otoliths, Indefinite Space, dadakuku, e·ratio, Utriculi*, and *M58*. His fiction has appeared in *Spoilage, Akkadian*, and *SoMa Literary Review*. He lives in Des Moines, Iowa with his wife and daughter.

Ron Ginzler's short fiction has appeared in *Chess Life, Tomorrowsf* and *Space & Time* magazines, and an anthology, *Feast of Laughter 5*. He has also published a collection of short stories, *The Iron Apples of the Stars*.

Jake Goldsmith is a writer with cystic fibrosis and the founder of The Barbellion Prize, a book prize for ill and disabled authors. He is the author of *Neither Weak Nor Obtuse* (SM, 2022), *In Hospital Environments: Essays on Illness and Philosophy* (SM, 2024), and *In Extremis* (SM, 2025).

Paul Griffiths is a Welsh writer, librettist, and music critic. A Chevalier dans l'Ordre des Arts et des Lettres, he is also a member of the American Academy of Arts and Sciences. His novel *Mr. Beethoven* was shortlisted for the 2020 Goldsmiths Prize. He lives on the Welsh coast.

Michael Hampton is a multimodal writer based in London, UK. He has been a reviewer for *Art Monthly* since 2009, and written extensively about artists' publishing. His critical study *Unshelfmarked: Reconceiving the artists' book* was published by Uniformbooks in 2015. *Against Decorum*, a hybrid collection of word reliefs and bibliographical fragments was published by information as material in 2022. *Paleodrafts*, a collaboration with Joe Devlin, was launched by N&B Press in 2023.

Ernest Hilbert is the author of the poetry collections *Sixty Sonnets, All of You on the Good Earth, Caligulan*—selected as winner of the 2017 Poets' Prize—and *Last One Out*. His fifth book, *Storm Swimmer*, was selected by Rowan Ricardo Phillips as the winner of the 2022 Vassar Miller Prize and appeared in 2023. He lives in Philadelphia.

Charles Holdefer is an American writer currently based in Brussels. His latest book is *Ivan the Terrible Goes on a Family Picnic* (SM, 2024).

DJ Huppatz lives in Naarm/Melbourne, Australia. He has published fiction in *Variant Literature, Menacing Hedge* and *Fugitives and Futurists*. Author of two poetry books, *Happy Avatar* (Puncher and Wattmann, 2015) and *Astroturfing for Spring* (Puncher and Wattmann, 2021), he also writes about design and architecture.

Carl Landauer taught history at Yale, Stanford, and McGill and is a contributing editor for *Poetry Flash* and a visiting scholar with UC Berkeley's Institute for South Asia Studies.

His poems—including his "refracted ekphrasis" poems on film adaptations of literature—have appeared in the *Kenyon Review*, *Exacting Clam*, *Poetry Flash*, and the Mary McCarthy Society website. His writing on poetry and cultural history has appeared in *Beat Scene*, *Salmagundi*, *The American Scholar*, *Confrontation*, *San Francisco Chronicle*, and *Renaissance Quarterly*—plus a critical analysis of Project 2025 published by Public Seminar.

Roy Lisker (1938–2019) was a writer, artist, mathematician, journalist and political activist. He was the author of a vast amount of literature in every imaginable form, which he largely self-distributed to friends and subscribers to his newsletter, *Ferment*. His conventionally published work includes *In Memoriam Einstein* (SM, 2016) and *Lincoln Center in July* (SM, 2016).

Jean Lorrain (1855–1906), born Paul Alexandre Martin Duval, was a French poet and novelist.

Kurt Luchs is a writer of poetry and prose who always hears voices but doesn't always do what they tell him. His latest book is *Tributaries: Essays & Verses Flowing from & Celebrating Favorite Poems* (SM, 2025).

Melissa McCarthy transmits from a tracking station in Edinburgh, Scotland. She's written *Photo, Phyto, Proto, Nitro* (SM, 2023) and *Sharks, Death, Surfers: An Illustrated Companion* (Sternberg, 2019).

Kat Meads' most recent book is *While Visiting Babette* (SM, 2025). Eons ago, she wrote a fan letter to Mavis Gallant in Paris and wonder of wonders she answered.

Brooke Mitchell is a queer poet on her way from northern Appalachia to New York City where she will begin attending NYU's MFA in creative writing. Find her work at *New York Quarterly*, *Santa Clara Review*, and more, including on her Substack: *Poems from the Notes App*.

Sonya Moor is a French and British author and translator of short fiction. Her collection *The Comet and Other Stories* is published by Cōnfingō, as is her translation of Albertine Sarrazin's *The Crib and Other Stories*. Her stories are widely published in literary reviews and anthologies, including *Best British Short Stories 2024* and *Best British Short Stories 2022*.

Fiona O'Connor lives in London. She has stories in *The Stinging Fly*, *The Lonely Crowd*, and *Sublunary Editions*. She produced open-air theatre at St. John's Mill, Dunloe, Co. Kerry, including the Irish premiere of Ramon del Valle-Inclan's *Divine Words*. She reviews for *The Morning Star*.

Ben Pester is a writer of long and short form fiction. His debut story collection *Am I in the Right Place?* was published in 2021, and was long listed for the 2022 Edge Hill Prize. His fiction and work has appeared in *Granta*, *The London Magazine*, *TANK*, *Hotel*, *Five Dials* and elsewhere. His debut novel *The Expansion Project* is published by Granta Books. He lives with his family in North London.

Jennifer M Phillips is a bi-national immigrant, painter, Bonsai-grower. Her chapbooks are *Sitting Safe In the Theatre of Electricity* (i-blurb.com, 2020) and *A Song of Ascents* (Orchard Street Press, 2022). With work in over 95 journals, she is currently a Pushcart Poetry Prize nominee.

Geoffrey Pitcher lives in southwestern France, where he gardens, cooks, and lingers in spots of time. When the weather is anything more promising than abysmal, he can be found at the shore, clamming and exploring.

Eric T. Racher lives in Riga, Latvia. His work has appeared in *Exacting Clam*, *Socrates on the Beach*, *minor literature[s]*, *Poetry Birmingham Literary Journal*, *ballast*, and elsewhere.

Nat Raum is a disabled artist, writer, and genderless disaster based on unceded Piscataway and Susquehannock land in Baltimore. They're the editor-in-chief of fifth wheel press. Their writing has been published with *Split Lip Magazine*, *BRUISER*, *beestung*, *Gone Lawn*, and others.

David Rose born 1949, resident in Britain, is now retired after a working life in the Post Office. His short stories are published widely in the UK and US, including in *The Penguin Book of the Contemporary Short Story* (ed. Philip Hensher, 2018) and partly collected in *Posthumous Stories* (Salt, 2013). He is the author of two novels: *Vault* (Salt, 2011) and *Meridian* (Unthank Books, 2015).

Shifra Sharlin has essays in *Salmagundi*, *Yale Review*, *Southwest Review*, *LA Review of Books*, *Raritan*, *New Letters*, and *The Contemporary Essay*, ed. P. Lopate, She taught and co-directed a course in reading and writing the modern essay as a Senior Lecturer at Yale until her retirement in 2022. She's a grandmother. Her cats died five years ago.

Mike Silverton is the author of *Anvil on a Shoestring* (SM, 2022), *Trios* (SM, 2023), and *Yoga for Pickpockets* (SM, 2024).

Hugo S. Simões comes from a small island along the Mid-Atlantic Ridge. He currently lives in Lisbon, Portugal. His poetry and prose have previously appeared in *Southwest Review*, *The Chicago Quarterly Review*, *Innisfree Poetry Journal*, and *MORIA*, among others.

Aug Stone is author of the comedy novels *The Ballad Of Buttery Cake Ass* and *Off-License To Kill*, the memoir *Nick Cave's Bar*, and the story collection *Sporting Moustances* (SM, 2024). His journalism has appeared in *The Quietus*, *The Comics Journal*, *Under The Radar*, and others sites and magazines. Aug was a founding member of H Bird and The Soft Close-Ups, and has played in countless other bands. He performs comedy as absurdist stream-of-consciousness raconteur, *Young Southpaw*.

Jocelyn Szczepaniak-Gillece teaches Film Studies at the University of Wisconsin-Milwaukee. Her strange fiction can be found in *Weird Horror*, *Apocalypse Confidential*, and *Sublunary Review*, among others.

Benjamin Wal is a writer living in Northampton, England. His stories have been shortlisted for the Galley Beggar Press Short Story Prize and the London Magazine Short Story Prize.

Eric Weiskott is a poet and scholar of poetry and poetics. His debut book of poetry is *Cycle of Dreams* (punctum books, 2024). Eric's poems appear in *Fence*, *Texas Review*, and *Inverted Syntax*. He lives in Massachusetts.

Jon Willer is a copywriter living in Brooklyn. His fiction has appeared in *Hawai'i Review*, *Juked*, *Knee-Jerk*, and *Paper Darts*.

Lawrence Winkler is a retired physician, traveler, and natural philosopher. He lives with Robyn on Vancouver Island and in New Zealand, tending their gardens and vineyards, and dreams. His writings have been published in *The Montreal Review* and other literary journals.

Addison Zeller lives in Wooster, Ohio, and edits fiction for *The Dodge*. His work has appeared in *3:AM*, *Epiphany*, *Cincinnati Review*, *minor literature[s]*, and many other publications.